Making Civics Relevant, Making Citizens Effective

Making Civics Relevant, Making Citizens Effective

Action Civics in the Classroom

Daniel Millenson, Molly Mills, and Sarah Andes

International Debate Education Association

New York, London & Amsterdam

Published by:
International Debate Education Association
105 East 22nd Street
New York, NY 10010

This book is published with the generous support of the Open Society Foundations.

Library of Congress Cataloging-in-Publication Data

Millenson, Daniel, author.
  Making civics relevant, making citizens effective : action civics in the classroom /
Daniel Millenson, Molly Mills, and Sarah Andes.
     pages cm
  ISBN 978-1-61770-068-2
  1. Civics--Study and teaching (Secondary)--United States. I. Mills, Molly, author. II.
Andes, Sarah, author. III. Title.
  LC1091.M58 2013
  370.11'5--dc23
                                    2013006077

Design by Kathleen Hayes

Printed in the USA

 IDEBATE Press

CONTENTS

Preface vii

Introduction 1

    The Generation Citizen Philosophy 1

    Generation Citizen's Core Values 2

    Generation Citizen's Program Goals 2

    Scope & Sequence 3

    Assessment 6

    Alignment with Standards 9

    Flexibility 9

    Grade-Level Adaptations 10

    Using the Generation Citizen Curriculum 10

LESSONS

Unit 1: Identifying Our Issue 15

    Lesson 1: Introduction to Civic Action 17

    Lesson 2: Community Issues 32

    Lesson 3: Choosing Our Focus Issue 40

    Lesson 4: Examining Evidence 49

    Lesson 5: From Root Cause to Goal 59

Unit 2: Planning Our Action 75

    Lesson 6: Identifying a Decision-Maker 77

    Lesson 7: Targeting Influencers 90

    Lesson 8: Selecting Tactics 97

Unit 3: Taking Action.. 109

    Lesson 9: Project Teams.. 110

    Lesson 9+: Taking Action Class Template................................ 118

Unit 4: Taking the Next Step 129

    Reflection and Next Steps.. 130

APPENDIXES

    Appendix A: Word of the Day Procedures 146

    Appendix B: Tactic Toolkit.. 147

        Lobbying.. 148

        Letters, Calls, and Emails 155

        Writing a Survey.. 162

        Holding a Public Meeting 167

        Holding a Coalition Meeting 172

        Using Social Media 181

        Writing an Op-Ed.. 188

        Writing a Media Advisory or Press Release.................. 194

        Writing a Letter to the Editor 202

    Appendix C: National Common Core Standards.................... 207

Preface

In 2007, *New York Times* columnist Thomas L. Friedman wrote a column titled "Generation Q" about Millennials and civic engagement. The "Q" stood for "quiet," because Friedman felt that the Millennials' admirable commitment to community and national service did not extend to the type of political activism necessary to addressing larger economic, social, and environmental problems in the United States and around the world. Too often, he argued, the "clicktivism" of Facebook "likes" and online petitions become not complements, but substitutes for the in-person activism and democratic participation ultimately necessary to effect real change. The mere 50 percent of young voters, aged 18–29, who voted in the 2012 presidential election would seem to underline the point: though this percentage was higher than in the 1990s, it was one of the lowest youth voting rates of any country in the world.

Whether or not you agree with Friedman's analysis (we think it a bit glib), it was not actually about "Millennials." Rather, it was about the narrow slice of Millennials who attend and graduate from (in this case, elite) universities—students who, according to the Center for Information & Research on Civic Learning and Engagement (CIRCLE) at Tufts University, are four to five times more likely to participate in civic affairs than someone without a high school diploma. And 42 percent of American youth do not continue their educations past high school. They, too, are citizens who need and deserve the ability to participate in our democracy, in their own self-government.

Too often, the media and even many educators confuse youth civic disengagement, especially low voter turnout rates, with disengagement from American politics or society. Yet, studies from CIRCLE, the Harvard Institute of Politics, and our own experience working with thousands of middle and high school students show that young people do care about their communities and our democracy. But apart from voting (a fairly minimal form of civic engagement), many young people do not know how to use democracy to make change on issues they care about, nor do they believe that their voices matter.

Scott Warren was a junior in college when he read Friedman's "Generation Q" article. It rankled him. As a leader in the movement to stop genocide in Sudan's Darfur region, he knew firsthand how effective young people could be in gaining media attention, shaping public opinion, and passing legislation.

In response to "Generation Quiet," in 2008 he created Generation Citizen (GC), a nonprofit organization devoted to empowering young people to become engaged and effective citizens. GC partners college student volunteers with classroom teachers to teach an action civics course in which teens solve problems they are facing in their own communities. Students lobby elected officials, write opinion pieces for newspapers, and make documentaries to advance solutions to important community issues. Through direct engagement in real-world advocacy, students gain the civic knowledge, skills, and motivation necessary to effect change in their communities. The organization concentrates on low-income and majority-minority schools in particular, because that is where what Meira Levinson of Harvard University calls the "civic empowerment gap" is greatest.

In early 2012, GC was approached by Martin Greenwald at the Open Society Foundations. While Martin was encouraged by GC's rapid growth—in the 2012-2013, the organization served 6,000 students in Boston, Providence, and New York City—Martin encouraged us to collate insights and observations from three years of implementing and revising our program to create a curriculum designed for classroom teachers outside the GC program who want to teach action civics—who want their students to learn about democracy by participating in it.

This book represents the results of those efforts. But it would not have been possible without the generous support of the Open Society Foundations. And our team had the support of another team of consultants and advisers and colleagues. John Zola, a former high school social studies teacher and professional developer extraordinaire, shared not just pedagogical practices and structural suggestions, but also contributed insights gleaned from years of teaching action civics courses in Boulder, Colorado. His willingness to probe every aspect of the curriculum, including its philosophical and structural underpinnings (to say nothing of his unfailing good humor), was invaluable. So, too, were the contributions of Pamela Gordon, a former social studies teacher in Boston and recent Harvard Graduate School of Education PhD. In addition to improving the lessons' pedagogical aspects, Pam helped create the portfolio assessment tools in this curriculum, enabling teachers to authentically gauge students' skills and understanding. We also owe a great debt to Meira Levinson of Harvard's Graduate School of Education, whose research and book *No Child Left Behind* have provided the underpinnings of the GC program and this curriculum. Meira graciously took time to help us plan a structure for the curriculum, and her edits on later drafts substantially improved it. Peter Levine, director of CIRCLE, and Bill Mendelsohn of Teach For America have also made significant contributions at various points in the process of conceiving and writing this book. Our editor, Eleanora von Dehsen, has provided vital guidance in creating a user-friendly curriculum that teachers anywhere in the United States can use. Our final acknowledgement goes to Scott Warren, Gillian Pressman, and Emily Falk of Generation Citizen. Scott, Gillian, and Emily shaped every aspect of this book with their incisive observations, constructive criticism, and patience and support.

Daniel Millenson, Molly Mills, and Sarah Andes
Brooklyn, New York, and Boston, Massachusetts

INTRODUCTION

Welcome to Generation Citizen's civics course. This curriculum will be the foundation for a powerful experience that empowers your students through an innovative pedagogical approach known as "action civics." It will allow them to effect change on issues they care about. Generation Citizen (GC) strengthens our nation's democracy by empowering young people to solve problems in their own communities through a rigorous course that teaches strategies for community action.

THE GENERATION CITIZEN PHILOSOPHY

Generation Citizen believes that the democratic system functions most effectively when it responds to the needs and desires of all of its citizens. Unfortunately, a growing body of evidence indicates that Americans do not understand the democratic process, do not trust it, and do not participate in it. That is in no small part because they have not been taught how to participate and how that participation can make a real difference in their everyday lives.

Although civic disengagement afflicts the entire American public, it is particularly pronounced among young people—especially low-income and minority young people. The consequence of this "Civic Engagement Gap" is that entire communities lack the civic knowledge, skills, and motivation to address vital issues they face. Our public schools—the very institution designed to prepare citizens for democracy—are not adequately providing low-income and minority youth the civics education they need to become engaged and effective citizens who can lead their communities.

Generation Citizen has, therefore, developed a course designed to help students gain the civic knowledge, skills, and outlook needed to start a dialogue about and to effect change on issues they care about; students learn civics by doing it. Accordingly, the action civics course—the heart of our program—promotes student agency and empowerment. The students—not the teacher—select the focus issue, plan how to take action on it, and then execute their plan. This student-centered approach is central to our curriculum.

Since effective citizenship relies on a set of civic skills, including persuasive written and oral communication, critical thinking, and group collaboration, Generation Citizen provides an academically rigorous framework for our course. The GC curriculum—like civics itself—is interdisciplinary and is, therefore, aligned with the Common Core standards, as well as relevant state standards in areas such as government, civics, and U.S.

history. Recognizing that an individual must be an educated person to be an effective citizen, the curriculum places a heavy emphasis on literacy and writing.

GENERATION CITIZEN'S CORE VALUES

Generation Citizen is unique not only because of our mission, but also because of the democratic values that underpin our efforts. We seek to ensure that these values permeate our organization's work—and this curriculum. The stakes could not be higher: how we educate our citizenry now will determine what type of society we will become. We, therefore, commit ourselves to the following principles throughout our work:

- **Grassroots Change.** *Every individual has a voice and the potential to change his or her community.* We believe all people play a role in the development of their communities and that meaningful change grows from local and personal knowledge. We work specifically with young people who have the chance and capacity to be life-long leaders and advocates.

- **Systemic Impact.** *We believe in big change, and always start at the root of the issue.* We address the root causes of problems instead of focusing on surface-level symptoms. Working through our democratic system of government is challenging, complex, and incremental—and necessary to create lasting change.

- **Collaboration and Diversity.** *Our differences make us stronger.* Our work is strengthened by incorporating multiple points of view into everything we do. We respect and embrace the diverse backgrounds, perspectives, insights, and experiences of our partners and believe that strong personal relationships allow us to best work and learn together.

- **Action.** *We learn by doing.* We believe that the process of *trying* can teach us as much as achieving our outcome. At the same time, we think carefully about the way things get done, and value learning from failure as much as celebrating success. We strive for our students to learn through experience so that they understand the process of effecting change and can apply it both now and in the future.

- **Open Mindedness.** *We are always learning and growing.* We do not have all of the answers, and there are many solutions. We must be curious, listen, reflect, make changes, and operate with humility in order to achieve our goals.

GENERATION CITIZEN'S PROGRAM GOALS

The Generation Citizen action civics course is designed to help students become engaged and effective citizens. We hope to expand and improve students' civic knowledge, civic skills, and civic outlook so that they can participate effectively in the democratic process. Each lesson has been crafted to meet one or more of the program goals.

Civic Knowledge

Civic knowledge is defined as a student's ability to grasp basic concepts of civic institutions and actors, which are taught throughout the course. This basic understanding of how the governmental process works is necessary to effectively become an engaged citizen.

Civic Skills

Civic skills are defined as those needed to effectively participate in the democratic process. These include developing a student's ability to analyze and examine issues and the ability to think critically about the role of an individual in a democratic society. Skills include oral and written persuasive communication, critical analysis, and group collaboration. We view these as necessary skills for effective participation in the political process as an engaged citizen.

Civic Outlook

Civic outlook is defined as a student's desire to actively participate in the political process and to take action on issues he or she cares about. These include a student's sense of social responsibility, civic agency and self-efficacy, and identity. Measuring students' motivation to participate in the political process and take action as democratic citizens is crucial to our goal of creating engaged young community leaders.

SCOPE & SEQUENCE

The Generation Citizen curriculum is laid out in a series of lessons designed to organize the progression of work, but it is also intended to be used flexibly depending on your preferences as well as the demands of the specific focus issue students choose.

The curriculum's organizing principle is Generation Citizen's approach to advocacy, as illustrated in the Advocacy Hourglass below. Students narrow down the set of potential community issues they could choose into one focus issue and, ultimately, one tightly defined goal. That goal then generates a set of targets that are, in turn, engaged through a larger number of tactics.

Advocacy Hourglass

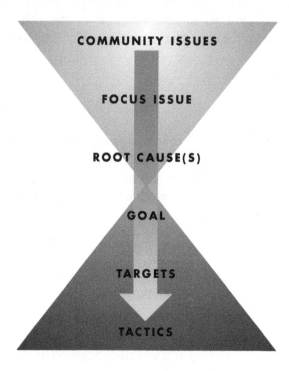

The curriculum is organized into four units that guide students through this process:

    Unit 1: Identifying Our Issue

    Unit 2: Planning Our Action

    Unit 3: Taking Action

    Unit 4: Taking the Next Step

At the beginning of each unit, we have summarized the main goals, activities, and sequence to follow.

The first nine lessons of the curriculum—which identify the students' issue and plan their action—are numbered sequentially; we recommend using them in this sequence (though they can be paced as needed to span more than one class period). The lessons are designed to provide ample flexibility and opportunities for variation. Each class will be different, with different focus issues and learning styles, so Generation Citizen offers a variety of options to best meet each class's needs.

Following Lesson 9, the curriculum changes form, and you become responsible for choosing the sequence of tactics that make the most sense for your students' project and action plan. An accompanying Tactic Toolkit helps you facilitate students learning how to utilize specific tactics. It is designed in skill-building segments, which can be taught to all or a portion of the class depending on the needs of different project teams.

Tactics are not all mandatory, and their relevance will depend on the action plan chosen by the class.

Accompanying each lesson are corresponding worksheets and, when appropriate, additional handouts and resources. These are referenced in the body of the lesson plan. They can be used to assess student progress, provide feedback, and gain insight into student interests in certain focus issue areas.

Curriculum Framework

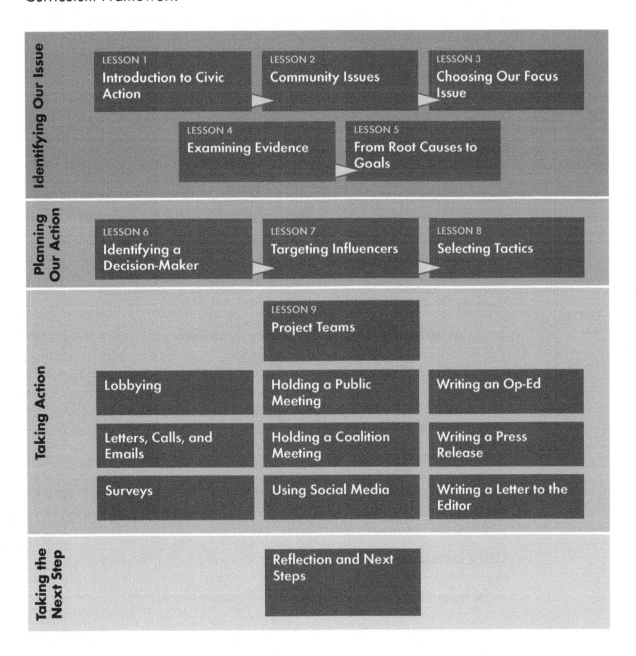

ASSESSMENT

Generation Citizen enables you to assess student progress through the use of the Generation Citizen (GC) Portfolio, a collection of student work that documents a student's growth in civic knowledge, civic skills, and civic outlook. These Portfolios are an opportunity for students to highlight the individual work they have contributed to the action plan process while also reflecting on their role in the class collaboration.

The GC Portfolio helps students and teachers assess student growth and learning as they relate to the program's overarching goals. Students reflect on their own learning over the course and see their development as civic actors. Students choose which of the tactics they used to implement the action plan they would like to include in their Portfolios. Giving students a voice in the Portfolio will help them feel ownership over the entire process.

With the exception of the sample tactic, which will likely be completed during Unit 3, the Portfolio assignments and assessments should be completed outside the lessons in the curriculum. They can be completed during class time or assigned as homework. We recommend that each student have two folders: "In-Progress GC" (for drafts, worksheets, and resource sheets they will refer to throughout the course and can use for future advocacy) and "Generation Citizen Portfolio" (for final products and assessments). At the end of the course, students can look through their "In-Progress" folder to find pieces for the Portfolio.

The Generation Citizen Student Portfolio includes:

1. **Table of Contents:** The contents page, created by students, lists and briefly describes all the pieces in their Portfolio.

2. **Introductory Letter:** Using guiding questions, students write letters of introduction to the instructor reflecting on their civic skills, knowledge, and current attitudes about civic participation before beginning the Generation Citizen curriculum. This will help you and the students see how they have progressed over the term when they write a final reflection. This letter should be assigned before you introduce Lesson 1 or during that lesson. If possible, read these letters before the second class.

3. **Unit 1 Assessment:** Using their worksheets and notes, students analyze a story of civic action and fill out the top part of the Generation Citizen Advocacy Hourglass. They are then asked to explain their diagram. The activity is designed to demonstrate an understanding of how to identify community issues, focus issues, and root causes, and how to determine a goal.

4. **Unit 2 Assessment:** Students are asked to fill out a tactics table based on a story of community action, recommend tactics to achieve a goal, and justify their choice. We recommend using this assessment as a mid-semester checkpoint.

5. **Tactics Example:** Students will choose one example of a tactic they have worked on to include in their Portfolio. This could be either a speaking or writing piece. Students include the first draft, the feedback they received, and a final draft of the product. In some cases, the final draft will be a group product.

6. **Group Collaboration Self-Assessment:** Students are asked to complete a self-assessment about the collaborative work they have done throughout the course.

7. **Final Assessment:** For the final assessment, students are asked to use everything they have learned in Generation Citizen and write an "instruction manual" for taking action and making change. This requires students to demonstrate their understanding of action planning.

8. **Final Reflection (Middle School) or Final Reflection (High School):** Students are asked to review their worksheets and Portfolio items and then write a reflection using examples from their Generation Citizen experience.

Portfolio Grading

You can assess students' Portfolios throughout the semester using a combination of rubrics and dialogue between you and your students. We include several types of assessment tools:

1. Three formal assessments that mirror a "traditional" quiz or test to measure civic skills and knowledge: Unit 1 Assessment, Unit 2 Assessment, and Final Assessment. Each of these assessments is accompanied by a rubric.

2. Two opportunities for students to reflect on their own learning: A Group Collaboration Self-Assessment and a Final Reflection on the student's experience with Generation Citizen and changing perspectives on civic engagement. Each of these assessments is accompanied by a rubric.

3. Three tactic rubrics (written persuasive communication, oral persuasive communication, and critical analysis) to help you assess one tactic selected by each student at the end of the term to include in his or her Portfolio.

4. A final Overall Portfolio rubric to assist you in assessing the thoroughness and quality of the full Portfolio.

The following table gives our recommendations for using these tools before, during, and after the course.

Portfolio Assessment Plan

Item	What This Is Assessing	How to Assess	Timeline/Notes
GC Introductory Letter	Civic outlook, knowledge, and skills	Teacher reads and responds to students with comments about how the course will push them to think about themselves as active citizens.	Before Lesson 2
Unit 1 Assessment	Civic knowledge and skills	Unit 1 Assessment Rubric	After Lesson 5
Unit 2 Assessment	Civic knowledge and skills	Unit 2 Assessment Rubric	After Lesson 8
Sample Tactic (from Unit 3)	Civic skills	Tactic rubrics that are completed at the time the pieces are completed.	After completion of Tactic and/or end of term
Group Collaboration Self-Assessment	Civic skills	Group Collaboration Rubric	Any time during Unit 3 (e.g., as an extended exit ticket)
Final Assessment	Civic knowledge and skills	Final Assessment Rubric	End of course
Final Reflection (Middle School) or Final Reflection (High School)	GC course and civic outlook	Final Reflection Rubric	End of course
Overall Portfolio	Overall student growth in the Generation Citizen course	Overall Portfolio Rubric	End of term

VOCABULARY INSTRUCTION

Vocabulary acquisition is critical to equip students with the communication skills and concepts necessary for effective democratic participation. To this end, the curriculum identifies key vocabulary terms through a Word of the Day, which comprises each lesson's "Do-Now." A Do-Now (sometimes known as a "Bell Ringer") should be on the board/on the projector before students enter the classroom each day (except the first lesson), and students should commence working on it as soon as they reach their desks, a routine that helps ensure that class time is maximized. The Do-Now should last approximately 3–5 minutes. We strongly advise using a timer so that the Do-Now does not encroach on the rest of the class time.

Generation Citizen provides a Word of the Day aligned to each day's instruction for Lessons 1–8. (See Appendix A for instructions on how to integrate the Word of the Day into the lesson.) In the less-standardized Units 3 and 4, you should select the Word of the Day for each period. We recommend selecting words that students will encounter in the course of their work, but that students would also encounter in other contexts. Avoid using technical terms as Word of the Day. For example, for most classes, "beneficial" would be a better Word of the Day than "appropriations."

ALIGNMENT WITH STANDARDS

Because Generation Citizen is an in-class experience, the curriculum is aligned with national academic standards, including the Common Core standards in English language arts and (for some focus issues) mathematics. The selected standards center on oral and written persuasive communication, reading and research, writing, listening and collaboration, and critical analysis of text and arguments. While we have highlighted a particularly aligned subset of standards in the Appendix, students may also improve in other areas of the overall sets of Common Core and other national and state standards.

Please see the relevant standards at the bottom of each lesson plan. Generation Citizen complements existing classroom material, while demonstrating the viability of civics as an effective interdisciplinary pursuit.

FLEXIBILITY

Generation Citizen encourages you to be creative with teaching strategies and supplementary content, while adhering to the core objectives, standards, and lesson sequence. While this curriculum strives to provide a universal template for successful civic action, we also recognize the variations in classroom contexts—from class size to students' backgrounds.

Please note that Generation Citizen assumes a class size of 25 for our lessons. Activities may need to be modified for classes that are significantly larger or smaller. We also assume a class period of 50 minutes. Therefore, whenever possible, we provide options for reducing or extending the lesson. We recognize, however, that some teachers may occasionally need to divide a lesson into two class periods or, for those on a block schedule, conduct two lessons in one class period.

Last, we want to stress that the activities and sample questions provided are intended merely as a means to a given end (the day's objective and the overall objectives of the course). Although designed with considerable thought and care, ours is neither a scripted curriculum nor a checklist; take advantage of the "teachable moment," the thought-provoking discussion, the relatable current event to enrich and enliven the Generation Citizen action civics course.

GRADE-LEVEL ADAPTATIONS

To accommodate middle school and high school students taking the GC program, we offer adaptations of various types for the curriculum.

- In each lesson, we have included both high school– and middle school–level national standards.

- Throughout the curriculum, we have noted optional adaptations to allow for differentiated use of the materials with students at various levels.

- In the Portfolio assessment, we have provided various differentiated assignments to measure learning for middle and high school students.

USING THE GENERATION CITIZEN CURRICULUM

Each lesson contains several components:

- **Overview** explains the purpose of the lesson and gives a brief snapshot of what students will experience in the lesson.

- Two-to-four **Objectives** outline what students should have accomplished by the end of the lesson.

- A **Word of the Day** and sample sentence to familiarize students with important vocabulary.

- **Materials** list of the resources you should gather and prepare before the class.

- **Preparation before Class** outlines what you must do before class starts.

- **Lesson**

  - **Introduction** presents the Do-Now and a student-friendly lesson overview giving students a context for what they will engage in during the lesson. The introduction might reference a past lesson or engage in a pre-lesson activity or discussion that is especially relevant to the objectives of the lesson. Time suggestions (assuming a 50-minute class period) are provided as a guideline.

  - **Sections** (typically given a heading pertinent to the content of the lesson) provide step-by-step directions for activities and products that students should complete to meet the objectives of the lesson. Time suggestions (assuming a 50-minute class period) are again provided as a guideline.

- **Conclusion** offers a wrap-up and/or exit ticket (a short formative assessment) that is designed to help students process what they have gained from the lesson and assess their learning. Giving students time to synthesize learning and reflect on the lesson is critical. Time suggestions (assuming a 50-minute class period) are again provided as a guideline.

- **Assessment** and, where appropriate, **Portfolio** assignments.

Each lesson also includes notes and suggestions to help you facilitate learning. The lessons can be adjusted, and you should feel free to adapt them to the needs of your class. Among the recurring features in the notes are:

- **Sample probing questions.** These appear where discussions can be made richer by encouraging students toward deeper thinking, alternative solutions, or more specific answers.

- **Exemplars/non-exemplars.** These illustrate the proper use of specific advocacy terms or elements (such as root cause or pressure points). You can also use them as examples to emulate or avoid. In general, exemplars demonstrate the language needed for successful completion of the day's objectives. In other cases, these exemplars/non-exemplars distinguish between accurate statements and incorrect or unfounded ones.

LESSONS

UNIT 1: IDENTIFYING OUR ISSUE

MAIN GOALS

At the end of Unit 1, students will be able to:
- analyze examples of different tactics for civic action in relation to sample goals;
- describe the advocacy framework of this action civics course;
- utilize and explain the purpose of small group work guidelines;
- identify issues in their communities and analyze them as public problems;
- utilize a consensus-bulding process to advocate for and discuss focus issues;
- use evidence to argue for a given focus issue;
- utilize democratic discussion guidelines to argue for and discuss focus issues;
- reach a consensus on a single focus issue;
- analyze print and online research on the root cause of their focus issue;
- evaluate evidence about the root cause as it relates to the local context for their focus issue;
- analyze and evaluate evidence provided by a guest speaker on the root cause of their focus issue (optional);
- select a root cause by analyzing its importance and feasibility;
- create a goal that addresses an identified root cause.

Students will have:
- analyzed how tactics change in relation to different goals;
- learned a framework for effective advocacy (the "Advocacy Hourglass");
- set guidelines for classroom interaction to enable productive discussion;
- identified and prioritized community issues;
- argued for and selected a class focus issue using a consensus-building process;
- analyzed and evaluated research (optional: and spoken with a community/issue expert) to determine the root cause of their focus issue;
- selected a root cause to address based on significance and feasibility;
- drafted a goal to address the chosen root cause.

UNIT SUMMARY

Lesson 1 begins by giving students examples of different tactics they can use to effect change, ranging from Facebook campaigns to direct lobbying. By ranking the effectiveness of tactics relative to sample goals, students begin to understand the connections between them. The class is then introduced to Generation Citizen's framework for advocacy, which will provide a map for the rest of the semester's planning and action. In Lesson 2, students work in small groups to generate, prioritize, and discuss issues that they want to address. In Lesson 3, students marshal evidence to argue for their preferred issue. After narrowing down the number of issues, students use a consensus-building process to determine what will be the "focus issue" for the entire class. In Lessons 4 and 5, students research and gather evidence on the root causes of their issue, examining print and online materials, and, if possible, hosting an issue or community expert in class. After identifying the most important root cause that is also feasible to address in the semester timeframe, students craft a goal statement to connect that cause to their desired impact on the focus issue.

LESSON 1: INTRODUCTION TO CIVIC ACTION

OVERVIEW

Students begin Lesson 1 by breaking into small groups to consider various tactics people use to effect change. They will order them from most to least effective in relation to sample goals, and then discuss their rankings. The opening activity will segue into a brief overview of the Advocacy Hourglass, which outlines the process the class will use for effecting change on the issue they choose.

OBJECTIVES

By the end of this lesson, students will be able to:

- analyze examples of different tactics for civic action in relation to sample goals;
- describe the advocacy framework of this action civics course;
- utilize and explain the purpose of small group work guidelines.

WORD OF THE DAY

Advocacy (noun): Getting support for a solution to a particular problem or for an idea or cause

Sample Sentence: Advocacy for equality by civil rights groups and individuals like Martin Luther King, Jr., led to the end of segregation.

> ### Note
> Appendix A outlines the procedure for integrating the Word of the Day into the lesson.

MATERIALS

- Resource sheet: Introducing Generation Citizen for each student

- Resource sheet: Small Group Guidelines for each student
- Worksheet: Advocacy Tactics for each student
- Worksheet: Advocacy Hourglass for each student
- Exit Ticket: Advocacy
- Portfolio: GC Introductory Letter

PREPARATION BEFORE CLASS

- Draw or print a large Advocacy Hourglass on chart paper. Keep it posted in your classroom throughout the course so students can refer to it as they move from step to step.
- Print a copy of the Portfolio assignment, resource sheets, worksheets, and exit ticket for each student.
- Write the Word of the Day and sample sentence on the board.

Note

Students should be given consistent instruction about whether they should keep worksheets and other materials (in a folder or binder) or whether they should submit them to you at the end of each period. Often, a lesson will require students to refer to work or materials from previous classes. (See Lesson 1: Conclusion for more information.)

To shorten this lesson

Have students write their GC Introductory Letters as homework before Lesson 1.

- Do today's exit ticket in another period or assign it for homework to be completed before the next class.
- Have students rank only 2 scenarios or give them only 4 tactic choices.

To enhance this lesson

Find a local specific case study of ordinary citizens, especially young people, employing the democratic process to have an impact on a local issue. Have small groups answer the following questions by analyzing the study:

- What was the problem?
- Why was the problem happening?
- What did they try to accomplish?
- What did they do to effect change?

LESSON

Introduction (10 minutes)

- *Do-Now:*

    Word of the Day: Advocacy

- *Lesson overview and framing*: Use the Introducing Generation Citizen resource sheet to briefly introduce the program and explain that today the class will begin discussing ways that students can bring about change on issues they care about.

Learning to Work in Small Groups (8 minutes)

- Explain that today the class will begin by working in small groups for this next activity and then will be reporting back as a whole class. Ask the class to respond orally to the following questions while you write their answers on the board:
    - When you have worked in small groups before?
    - What makes this successful?
    - What are problems that you've encountered in this arrangement?
- Explain that students often will be working in small groups and should use a few guidelines to ensure that they can collaborate with each other as much as possible. Distribute Small Group Guidelines and review.

Ranking Activity (17 minutes)

- Break students into groups of 4–5.
- Explain that to complete this activity, they need to know what the word "effective" means.

    Effective (adjective): Successfully does what was meant to be done/planned

    Sample Sentence: Detention was an effective punishment for fighting in class because it made students think twice about doing it again.

- Distribute an Advocacy Tactics worksheet and discuss the Word of the Day. Explain that each lesson will include a Word of the Day and that from now on students should begin working on it as soon as they reach their desks.
- Review each tactic. Explain that each tactic is an example of a way to effect change on a particular issue.
- Tell the groups that, using small group techniques, they will analyze three different issue scenarios and decide how they would rank the tactics from the most effective to least effective in addressing each issue. Ask the groups to choose a member who will verbally share the decisions they made with the class.
- Have students do a ranking round for each of the three scenarios on the worksheet.

1. Students in the community don't have access to up-to-date and accurate information about job openings and can't find employment.

2. Police often stop and frisk students on the street, even if they aren't doing anything wrong.

3. The school has few or no sports teams or after-school clubs.

- Give the groups 5 minutes to rank the tactics for the first scenario.

- While the groups determine their rankings, walk around and question them when needed to ensure that they are abiding by the small group procedures and creating a fully ranked list.

- At the end of the 5-minute round, have one student from each group respond to the following questions. Note their answers on the board.

  - Which method did you rank as most effective? Why?

  - Which method did you rank as least effective? Why?

- Repeat the process for the final 2 scenarios.

Sample probing questions

- Who would see and care about that tactic?

- How many people would be convinced by it?

- How would you explain what makes something ineffective?

Process of Effecting Change (10 minutes)

- At the end of the ranking rounds, lead a discussion about the group's responses. Students should feel free to disagree as long as they make an argument for the methods they selected. You might use the following questions:

  - What do you notice about the rankings? (e.g., They differ at least somewhat for each issue.)

  - Why do you think that the rankings were different in different groups or for the different scenarios? (e.g., Different actions are more or less effective depending on the issue you're addressing.)

- Explain that one way to initiate change is advocacy and that all the tactics they have just examined are part of advocacy. This is what they will be learning to do—and actually doing—in the course. Refer back to the Word of the Day.

- Explain that if you pick the right tactics, you can begin and carry through the process of real change on an issue.

- Distribute Advocacy Hourglass worksheet and refer to the large Advocacy Hourglass you have posted in the room.

Advocacy Hourglass

- Explain that this is a visual way to show how to do advocacy and to plan how to effect change. Label each section of the chart and have students copy the labels and the short definitions into the Advocacy Hourglass on their worksheets.

  - *Community Issues*: the range of problems/issues in the neighborhood and school (e.g., anything from homelessness to safety)

  - *Focus Issue*: the problem/issue you care most about that we'll work on this semester

  - *Root Causes*: the reasons *why* this problem/issue is happening/going on (e.g., Students are not signing up for the SAT because no one teaches them how to do so.)

  - *Goal*: the impact we'll make on the focus issue by addressing/fixing a root cause

  - *Targets*: the major influential people or groups who can help accomplish a goal (e.g., Our decision-maker, others who can influence the decision-maker, etc.)

  - *Tactics*: the actions taken to convey your messages to targets (e.g., Set up a meeting, write a newspaper article, organize an assembly, etc.)

- Explain that the Advocacy Hourglass reflects the process *they* will use to initiate change on an issue in *their* community—whether city, neighborhood, or school—this semester. Explain that you are here to guide them in the process of determining what the most effective actions will be to address problems the class identifies.

- In Generation Citizen, they will choose a problem that *they* care about and use advocacy to help address it. Advocacy allows *anyone*, student or adult, to move change forward in our democracy.

Sample probing questions

- Can you think of an issue where a tactic might switch from effective to ineffective?

- Does anyone disagree or have a different opinion?

CONCLUSION (5 minutes)

- Distribute 2 folders to each student. Have students label one folder "Portfolio." They will use these to store their Portfolio elements and eventually will submit the entire Portfolio to you at the end of the term for grading.

- Have students label the other "In-Progress GC." They will use this folder to keep worksheets, ongoing drafts, and items that they may choose later to add to their formal Portfolio. Tell students to bring this folder with them to class every day or leave it in a designated place in the classroom.

- Distribute and review GC Introductory Letter. Remind students that their letters will become part of their Portfolios.

- Tell the students to write their name on each folder.

- Distribute the exit ticket. Explain that an exit ticket is a brief set of questions that will give them an opportunity to reflect on the day's learning and you a sense of what students have learned. Call on a student to read the exit ticket out loud or do this yourself.

- Explain that addressing a problem starts by deciding which problems matter most to us and are worth our time. In response to this statement, have students complete their exit tickets and submit them to you.

- Tell students to keep their worksheets in their In-Progress GC folder or submit them to you for grading before they put them in their folder.

Note

Stand by the door to collect the exit tickets and the introductory letters (if these were assigned before Lesson 1).

ASSESSMENT AND PORTFOLIO ELEMENTS

Exit Ticket: Advocacy

Use one sentence to answer each of the following questions:

- What would you change if you were in charge of your school?
- What would you change if you were in charge of your neighborhood/city?

Portfolio: GC Introductory Letter. This Portfolio element should be assigned to and completed independently by students before Lesson 2.

COMMON CORE STANDARDS

- SL.8.1.a-d
- SL.8.6
- SL.9-10.1.a-d
- SL.9-10.6

Introducing Generation Citizen

Generation Citizen is built on the conviction that students can create change in their communities.

- This written curriculum is based on a program more than 10,000 students in Greater Boston MA, Providence, RI, and New York City completed between 2011 and 2013. By participating in Generation Citizen, you are joining a national movement of young people who are working to improve their communities.

- In Generation Citizen, you identify an issue in your community that you want to address. In the past, students have worked on community issues such as gang violence, teen pregnancy, public transportation, and homelessness, and school issues such as school nutrition, recycling, and bullying. Later in the term, your class will decide on your own focus issue.

- Generation Citizen's action civics program is about getting to the root of a problem. Generation Citizen is about creating cures, not just applying Band-Aids. It's the difference between volunteering at a homeless shelter and lobbying to change housing policies so that fewer people are homeless or the difference between picking up litter in a park and creating a trash removal program so that litter doesn't happen in the first place.

- Generation Citizen is about working together to create change. In a democracy such as ours, every person is responsible for being an engaged and informed participant so that, together, we can achieve great things.

Small Group Guidelines

When in a small group, make sure:

- Your desks or chairs are arranged to directly face one another, are close together so you can hear one another, and your group is not too close to any other groups.

- You are listening to your classmates to understand, make your ideas clearer, and develop your thinking. You should ask questions that help you and your group members do this productively.

- Your body language and attitude show listening and respect.

- Every member in the conversation has a voice and is invited to speak and share.

- Every member of the group asks questions and pushes the group's thinking.

- Everyone speaks thoughtfully—avoid saying "... and stuff" or "... blah, blah."

When in a small group, your job is to:

- have the attitude of "I want to learn" and "I want to teach others";

- use your curiosity to make connections between new and old learning;

- participate for the sake of your own learning—not just to perform for a grade;

- care about the learning of everyone else.

Sentence starters to help your conversation:

- Can we think of another example?

- Tell me more about _____.

- Explain your thinking about ____.

- Why might someone disagree with us? What could we say?

WORKSHEET

Advocacy Tactics

DO-NOW

Word of the Day: _____

Definition: _____

_____

_____

_____

Sample Sentence: _____

_____

_____

_____

My Sentence: _____

_____

_____

_____

Favorite Pick: _____

_____

_____

_____

ACTIVITY

Instructions: As a group, decide how you would rank the tactics from the most effective (1) to least effective (6) way of beginning the process of change for each of the three problems listed.

Scenario 1: Students in the community don't have access to up-to-date and accurate information about job openings and can't find employment.

Rank	Tactic
	Meet in person with a decision-maker (example: mayor, school principal)
	Organize a protest/rally
	Create a Facebook page/group
	Hold a neighborhood meeting/school assembly
	Create a documentary movie
	Write a newspaper article

Ranking

- Which method did you rank as most effective? Why?

- Which method did you rank as least effective? Why?

Scenario 2: Police often stop and frisk students on the street, even if they aren't doing anything wrong.

Rank	Tactic
	Meet in person with a decision-maker (example: mayor, school principal)
	Organize a protest/rally
	Create a Facebook page/group
	Hold a neighborhood meeting/school assembly
	Create a documentary movie
	Write a newspaper article

Ranking

- Which method did you rank as most effective? Why?

- Which method did you rank as least effective? Why?

Scenario 3: The school has few or no sports teams or after-school clubs.

Rank	Tactic
	Meet in person with a decision-maker (example: mayor, school principal)
	Organize a protest/rally
	Create a Facebook page/group
	Hold a neighborhood meeting/school assembly
	Create a documentary movie
	Write a newspaper article

Ranking

- Which method did you rank as most effective? Why?

- Which method did you rank as least effective? Why?

WORKSHEET

Advocacy Hourglass

OVERVIEW

This Advocacy Hourglass is a tool that will guide how the class builds their action plan. You can use it again whenever you want to build other plans to initiate change or take action.

Instructions: Follow along with your teacher's description of each part of the following Advocacy Hourglass. Copy the labels and the short definitions into the space below.

Parts of Advocacy Hourglass   Definitions

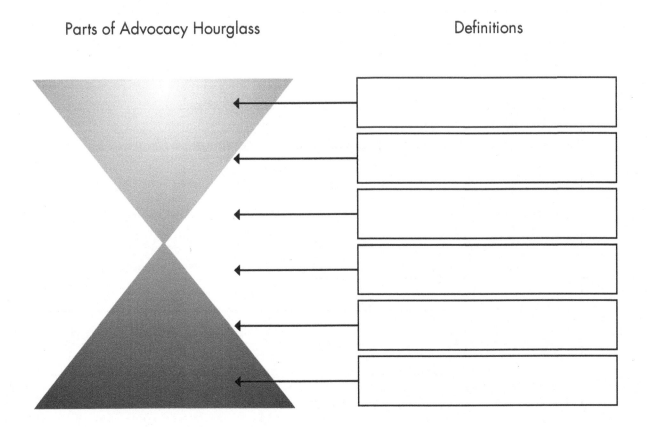

EXIT TICKET

Advocacy

Instructions: Write your response below and hand this to your teacher at the end of class.

Use one sentence to answer each of the following questions.

- What would you change if you were in charge of your school?

_____

_____

_____

_____

_____

_____

- What would you change if you were in charge of your neighborhood/city?

_____

_____

_____

_____

_____

_____

PORTFOLIO

GC Introductory Letter

Instructions: Write a letter to your teacher answering the questions below. You may answer them in whatever order you wish. Middle school students only need answer the first five questions.

1. Who are you? What is important to you?

2. What was your most meaningful experience in school last year? Why? (It can be a project you did, something you learned that has stayed with you, etc.)

3. Describe your community. (You may choose to write about your school, neighborhood, or city.)

4. What do you consider to be the three most pressing problems facing our communities today? (You may choose to write about neighborhood, city, state, national, or global problems.)

5. Do you think young people can be involved in and influence politics and government? Why or why not?

6. What does it mean to you to be a citizen/resident of your community?

7. Anything else your teacher may find interesting about you.

LESSON 2: COMMUNITY ISSUES

OVERVIEW

Students will identify issues that they consider problems in their community. As a class, they will discuss these issues and begin to prioritize them.

OBJECTIVES

By the end of this lesson, students will be able to:

- identify issues in their community and analyze them as public problems;
- utilize small group discussion guidelines to advocate for and discuss focus issues.

WORD OF THE DAY

Issue (noun): An important topic or problem that can be discussed/debated

Sample Sentence: The biggest issue at Monique's school was the tardy policy; teachers and students argued about the fairness of detentions for being late.

MATERIALS

- Worksheet: Community Issues
- Exit Ticket: Issues

PREPARATION BEFORE CLASS

- Post the Advocacy Hourglass if it is not already at the front of the class.
- Print a worksheet and exit ticket for each student.
- Write the Word of the Day and sample sentence on the board.
- Write the following questions on the board:
  - What would you change if you were in charge of your school?
  - What would you change if you were in charge of your neighborhood/city?
  - What would make your school better?
  - What would make your neighborhood/city better?

LESSON

Introduction (8 minutes)

- *Do-Now:*

     Word of the Day: Issue

- *Lesson overview and framing:* Explain that the class discussed three scenarios in which people saw problems and decided to take various types of action to address these problems—this is advocacy. Today, the class will begin thinking about what they consider to be problems in their community so they can gather ideas about what might become the focus of their own civic action (the focus issue).

Identifying Possible Community Problems (15 minutes)

- Review the Advocacy Hourglass structure and its purpose.

- Explain that the class will be starting on the first section of the hourglass: talking about community issues. Over the course of the next several lessons, they will narrow the list to 1 focus issue. Ask students for ideas about why the class should choose just 1 issue. (e.g., It takes a team/group of people to effect change. Or, if we try to do too much at once, we won't be good at any of it.)

- Using Small Group Guidelines, lead the students in a brief review of how to talk in a group. Ask for a few student suggestions on what leads to good and bad discussions. (e.g., Good = "Can you explain? Bad: "That's stupid. You're wrong.")

- Explain that, in small groups, students will think about and discuss the major issues facing their community (whether that's their school, neighborhood, or the entire city). Distribute the worksheet and tell the class that before they have this discussion everyone is to complete the questions on the sheet.

Note

If students are having trouble coming up with issues, ask questions to expand their thinking and solicit more responses based on the initial suggestions they have made.

> *For example:* If the issue were bullying: What do you mean by bullying? Are students getting beaten up? Or are you talking about nasty messages on Facebook? If students are getting beaten up: Where is it happening?

Only by tightly defining the problem will we be able to craft a solution. If community issues aren't concrete and specific, the focus issue won't be either—and then the class won't be able to understand root causes or create a quality action plan. Make sure that you ask questions to find out exactly what they are experiencing, seeing, or hearing about.

Prioritizing the Problem (25 minutes)

- Divide the students into groups of 4 and explain that for this activity each group member will have a specific role. These roles are:

  - The "asker" calls on each member of the group to give answers to the questions.
  - The "writer" writes down the responses that each member shares and the reason each person gives for his or her answer.
  - The "ranker" then facilitates a discussion about each answer to help the group determine which 2 issues they consider most important.
  - The "reporter" will announce to the whole class what the group's top 2 issues are and explain their choices.

- Give students 1 minute to choose their roles. Then tell the "asker" to start the discussion.

- Circulate during the activity. Ask probing questions to guide students in determining what issues they seem most concerned about and what the specific problems are.

- Ask the students to reconvene as a whole class. Have the "reporter" from each group announce the top 2 issues and explain the group's reasoning for the choice. Write these on the board.

- Host a class discussion of the answers. You may guide the conversation using the following questions:

  - Which of these issues concerns you most right now, and why? Tell me about a time when you saw this problem. Give me an example.
  - Which of these issues seems to be the biggest problem you or other people are facing, and why? Who is affected by the problem and who would benefit from having this issue addressed?
  - Which of these issues, if we addressed it successfully, would most improve your life or the lives of the people affected?

Guide students away from a discussion of feasibility of the project at this point. (They will consider feasibility at a later stage.) Remind them that using the Advocacy Hourglass will help them create a good plan. Explain that this is their opportunity to argue for the issues they think matter most.

Exemplar issue language

- Students are regularly getting mugged at the bus stop across the street from the school.
- Students have to pay full fare for subway/bus passes even if they live far from school, resulting in financial strains for families and unnecessary tardiness/absences.
- High school females who are pregnant/have had kids are more likely to drop out.

CONCLUSION (5 minutes)

- Preview what they will be doing in the next class.
- Explain that the class will not be able to take action on all the issues they have raised, so you will take their exit tickets home to tally up the top 3 or 4 issues in preparation for choosing the focus issue during the next class.
- Instruct students to keep their worksheets in their In-Progress GC folder or submit them to you first for grading.
- Have students complete the exit ticket and submit it to you.

ASSESSMENT AND PORTFOLIO ELEMENTS

Exit Ticket: Issues

On a separate sheet of paper, write the top two issues you care most about (either that you suggested or heard from another group today).

Note

Ensure that students have time to complete this exit ticket. It is a critical step in selecting the focus issue in Lesson 3.

Take these exit tickets home and tally them to narrow the options to 3-to-4 top potential issues.

COMMON CORE STANDARDS

- SL.8.1.a-d
- SL.8.6
- SL.9-10.1.a-d
- SL.9-10.6

WORKSHEET

Community Issues

DO-NOW

Word of the Day: _____

Definition: _____

_____

_____

_____

Sample Sentence: _____

_____

_____

_____

My Sentence: _____

_____

_____

_____

Favorite Pick: _____

_____

_____

_____

OVERVIEW AND OBJECTIVES

In this lesson, you will identify issues that you consider to be problems in your community. You will first discuss these issues in your group and then begin to prioritize them as a class.

By the end of this lesson, you will be able to:

- identify issues in your community and analyze them as public problems;

- utilize small group discussion guidelines to advocate for and discuss focus issues.

ACTIVITY

Instructions:

1. Independently, answer the following questions to identify issues that matter to you:

   - What would you change if you were in charge of your school?

     _____

     _____

   - What would make your school better?

     _____

     _____

   - What would you change if you were in charge of your neighborhood/city?

     _____

     _____

   - What would make your neighborhood/city better?

     _____

     _____

2. Assign each member of your group a role.

   - The "asker" calls on each member of the group to give answers to the questions.

   - The "writer" writes down the responses that each member shares and the reason each person gives for his or her answer.

- The "ranker" then facilitates a discussion about each answer to help the group determine which two issues they consider most important.

- The "reporter" will announce to the whole class what your group's top 2 issues are and explain your choices.

3. Have the asker begin the discussion.

To argue for a topic, address the following questions:

- Why does this issue matter?

- Who in our community is affected by it and why/how is it a problem?

- Why should we choose this issue over others?

As your group presents suggestions, the writer takes notes. Once the discussion is finished, the writer passes her notes to the ranker so that he can facilitate a discussion to reach agreement on what the group sees as most important two issues. Make sure to justify your rankings so the reporter can explain them to the class.

Final Top Two Issues

1. _____

_____

2. _____

_____

EXIT TICKET

Issues

Instructions: List the two issues you care most about (either that you suggested or heard from another group today). Hand this to your teacher as you leave.

Top Two Issues

1. _____

_____

2. _____

_____

COMMUNITY ISSUES

FOCUS ISSUE

ROOT CAUSE(S)

GOAL

TARGETS

TACTICS

LESSON 3: CHOOSING OUR FOCUS ISSUE

OVERVIEW

Students will use consensus-building guidelines to discuss and decide on their class focus issue, which they will work on for the rest of the course.

OBJECTIVES

By the end of this lesson, students will be able to:
- use evidence to argue for a given focus issue;
- utilize a consensus-building process to argue for and discuss focus issues;
- reach a consensus on a single focus issue.

WORD OF THE DAY

Consensus (noun): A general agreement/decision by a group of people

Sample Sentence: When Juan's parents saw his report card, they talked to each other and came to a consensus: no more video games until he got all As and Bs.

MATERIALS

- Worksheet: Choosing Our Focus Issue
- Exit Ticket: Choosing Our Focus Issue
- Slips of paper for each student

PREPARATION BEFORE CLASS

- Tally the focus issue suggestions from the previous class to determine the 3–4 with the most votes. If necessary, combine or adjust similar topics to narrow options to 3–4.
- Post the Advocacy Hourglass if it is not already at the front of the class.

- Familiarize yourself with the Building Consensus chart on p. 44.
- Print a worksheet and an exit ticket for each student.
- If possible, arrange class seats in a circle for this day.
- Write the Word of the Day and sample sentence on the board.

Note

Upcoming Guest Speaker

To prepare for the guest speaker recommended in Lesson 5, begin to solicit potential speakers as soon as students decide on a focus issue. See Guest Speaker Invitation and Briefing Guide (p. 58) for details.

To shorten this lesson

- Do today's exit ticket in another period or assign it for homework to be completed before the next class.
- Use your discretion on whether there are 3–4 top issue choices or whether to narrow the choice to 2–3. If so, only report the top 2–3.

LESSON

Introduction (8 minutes)

- *Do-Now:*

    Word of the Day: Consensus

- *Lesson overview and framing:* Explain that today is a major day because the class will be choosing the issue that they will focus on for the rest of the course. This is a difficult decision to make and will require all students to contribute their ideas and listen to those of others. One reason a democracy is so important is that you can get more ideas on the table and, therefore, come up with better solutions to problems. Explain that to make sure all good ideas are heard, the class will use a process that will ensure that they don't miss any ideas and will reach a decision that is best for the group.

Discussing Our Decision Process (8 minutes)

- Explain that you have tallied the suggestions that students made in their exit tickets during the previous class and come up with the 3-4 that received the most votes.

Explain your process for narrowing, especially how you may have combined some topics. Talk about how some students will not see their issue in this list and that the challenge they now face will be to determine how they can make the remaining issues work for them. Share the results of your tally and write them on the board. Remind students of the Advocacy Hourglass to show how they are moving to the stage where they choose the focus issue.

- Explain that because today's decision will shape the rest of the program, the class will need to consider what issue would be the strongest choice for them to pursue. While no issues are "bad," the class needs to determine which is most feasible for them to address so that they can actually get change in motion.

Note

Optional: Ask if any students want to give a 30-second explanation of why they strongly support any of the issues you listed.

Point out that students will be able to apply what they learned in working on this issue to future advocacy.

Narrowing the Issues (5 minutes)

- Explain that to ensure that everyone has a chance to express his or her views on an issue, the class will use a secret ballot to narrow the issue to 2 options. This process will NOT determine the final topic but will help class members see what others are thinking before they make their final discussion.

- On a scrap piece of paper, have each student write his or her top choice and submit it to you. You or a student volunteer should tally the results as quickly as possible.

Consensus-Building Process (5 minutes)

- Explain that the class will use the results of the tally to start a consensus-building conversation. In working to create a consensus, the class is trying to find a topic to which everyone can commit even if it is not her or his personal choice.

- *For high school students:* Draw a T-chart on the board like the one below to explain the difference between consensus-building and voting. Put consensus on one side and voting on the other. Ask students to briefly discuss the following question to help fill out the chart:

  What do you think are the advantages and disadvantages of using consensus instead of voting for a focus issue?

Direct Voting		Consensus-Building	
Pro (+)	Con (–)	Pro (+)	Con (–)
• speed • legitimacy • clear cut • easy with groups	• win/lose • divisive • less discussion • difficult to get buy-in • simplifies issues as black and white	• more voices heard • broader buy-in • encourages compromise • encourages creativity • everyone must participate	• slow • messy • complicated • no single 'winner' • can mean a lot of compromise

- Explain that students can express their opinions in certain ways to help make finding consensus easier. Distribute the worksheet and discuss the options under Building Consensus. Remind students that for consensus-building to work, they must be willing to compromise and even change their minds.

Making Our Choice (25 minutes)

- Announce the results of the tally and use the Building Consensus chart on p. 44 to explain the process.
- Move through Phases 1, 2, and 3 as appropriate.
- Announce the final issue that the class will focus their action on during this term.

CONCLUSION (5 minutes)

- Preview what the class will be doing in the next class. Explain that the next few classes will help them move from determining their focus issue to action. Point out the next step on the Advocacy Hourglass, where they will learn more about the focus issue so they can understand the causes of the problem.
- Instruct students to keep their worksheets in their In-Progress GC folder.
- Distribute the exit ticket. Call on a student to read the exit ticket prompt out loud or do this yourself.
- Have students complete the exit ticket and submit it to you.

Building Consensus

PHASE 1	PHASE 2	PHASE 3
(getting agreement on initial vote for 2 issues)	(comparing 2 issues)	(decision on 1 issue)
Say "It sounds like these two are the most compelling issues for our class. Our first step will be to see if we can agree to narrow these down to 1."	Go around the circle and give students a chance to use one of the following responses for EACH of the two topics during their turn. Write their responses down either on the board or paper as a tally or notes.	Say "It sounds like more people are more strongly supportive of _____ issue. In order to get as close to consensus as possible, I am going to propose that we focus on that topic this term so we can make sure as many people as possible are invested."

Ask that if any student feels they cannot live with any of the remaining 2 options that they respond using the following response: "I can't live with any of these because _____."	Response options: "Yes I am excited about any of those", "Yes I can live with any of those", "I'm not thrilled but I can go along", "Here is what I would need to be willing to do this _____", "I can't live with any of these because _____."	Go around the circle and have students use one of the following responses: "Yes I am excited about that", "Yes I can live with that", "Here is what I would need to be willing to do this _____", "I can't live with that because _____."

If there is no major disagreement based on the initial vote to narrow to 2 options from the original secret tally, remove the other options from visibility to refocus the class on the remaining options.	If students respond with "Here is what I would need" or "I can't live with this," ask them to explain their answer further and suggest adaptations to the focus issues to see if they can move to "I'm not thrilled but I can go along" or "I can live with those."	If students respond with "Here is what I would need" or "I can't live with this" ask them to explain their answer further and suggest adaptations to the focus issue to see if they can move to "I'm not thrilled but I can go along" or "I can live with those."

ASSESSMENT AND PORTFOLIO ELEMENTS

Exit Ticket: Choosing Our Focus Issue

What are two-to-three things you would like to learn about our focus issue?

COMMON CORE STANDARDS

- SL.8.1.b
- WHST.6-8.8
- RH.6-8.5
- SL.9-10.1.b
- WHST.9-10.8
- RH.9-10.5

WORSHEET

Choosing Our Focus Issue

DO-NOW

Word of the Day: _____

Definition: _____

_____

_____

_____

Sample Sentence: _____

_____

_____

_____

My Sentence: _____

_____

_____

_____

Favorite Pick: _____

_____

_____

_____

OVERVIEW AND OBJECTIVES

You will use a consensus-building process to discuss and decide on your class focus issue, which you will work on for the rest of the course.

By the end of this lesson, you will be able to:

* use evidence to argue for a given focus issue;

* utilize a consensus-building process to argue for and discuss focus issues;

* reach a consensus on a single focus issue.

Building Consensus

During this lesson, your class will be using a consensus-building process to decide on 1 issue they will work on this term. Your teacher will explain the process. Below are options for your responses during the conversation. Use these as guidelines to help you frame your answers during each round.

Options:

* "Yes, I am excited about any of those."

* "Yes I can live with any of those."

* "I'm not thrilled but I can go along."

* "Here is what I would need to be willing to do this _____."

* "I can't live with any of those because _____."

Remember that you cannot say "I can't live with any of these" without providing an explanation.

EXIT TICKET

Choosing Our Focus Issue

Instructions: Write your response to the following question below. Hand this in to your teacher at the end of class.

What are two-to-three things you would like to learn about the focus issue?

1. _____

_____

2. _____

_____

3. _____

_____

LESSON 4: EXAMINING EVIDENCE

OVERVIEW

Students will examine and analyze evidence about their focus issue to determine its root cause, which will shape their goal and action plan.

OBJECTIVES

By the end of this lesson, students will be able to:

- analyze print and online research on the root cause of their focus issue;
- evaluate evidence about the root cause as it relates to the local context of their focus issue.

WORD OF THE DAY

Root cause (noun): The origin of a problem; the basic/fundamental reason a problem exists

Sample Sentence: Keisha argued that the root cause of all the garbage on her street is that there aren't enough trashcans. If there were, she thought, people wouldn't litter.

MATERIALS

- Worksheet: Examining Evidence
- Exit Ticket: Examining Evidence
- Variety of research materials (see Preparation Before Class for specifics)
- Guest Speaker Briefing Guide

PREPARATION BEFORE CLASS

- Gather research about potential root causes of your class's focus issue. Try to find enough information so that each small group of 4–5 students has a different resource. Make sure the reading levels are appropriate for the class. This research should:

- focus on information about the *cause* of the problem, not just the symptoms. This may be contained in evidence about how others have addressed this problem;
- include content in various representations (figures/charts, primary/secondary sources, statistics and narrative);
- reflect a variety of views on the issue's root cause;
- have locally specific content as much as possible.

- Read and familiarize yourself with the evidence and prepare to answer the questions listed in the lesson below.
- Print a worksheet and an exit ticket for each student. Print enough copies of the evidence so that each student in a group has a copy.
- Arrange classroom seats into small-group clusters of 4–5 students.
- Post the Advocacy Hourglass if it is not already at the front of the class.
- Write the focus issue on the board.
- Write the Word of the Day and sample sentence on the board.
- Draw the following chart on the board. Adjust the number of evidence columns for the number of Learning Groups you have.

	Evidence _____	Evidence _____	Evidence _____
What does this article/evidence say is the problem?			
What information does the research use to prove this is a problem?			
According to the article/evidence, why is this problem happening?			
Compare/contrast this article to our school/ neighborhood. What is different? What applies to our situation?			

> **Note**
>
> Lesson 5 calls for you to invite a guest speaker to class (see the Guest Speaker Invitation and Briefing Guide on p. 58). If you are able to secure a speaker earlier, you can have him or her speak in Lesson 4 and then use print/online evidence in Lesson 5.
>
> The variety and quality of research here are critical to the successful framing and understanding of the issue for your students.

> **To shorten this lesson**
>
> - Assign today's exit ticket as homework to be completed before the next class.
> - Skip the jigsaw activity and move from small group article analysis into full group discussion where you complete the chart on the board.

LESSON

Introduction (8 minutes)

- *Do-Now:*

  Word of the Day: root cause

- *Lesson overview and framing:* Reference the Advocacy Hourglass. Remind students that they are now going to work on the third part of the advocacy process: looking for the root cause.

- Explain that to effectively address the focus issue, the class needs to know the cause of the problem. If we don't know what's causing the problem, we can't solve it. To find the root cause of the problem, the class needs to analyze evidence. This analysis will also help them later when they try to win support for their action.

- *For middle school students:* Have students copy the following definition of "evidence" on their worksheet and then ask them to complete in their own words the sentence stem "Evidence is _____."

- Definition: Facts and information that tell us if something is true or not.

- Sample Sentence: The high unemployment rate was only 1 piece of evidence pointing to the troubles the community was having.

- If you are inviting a guest speaker for Lesson 5, explain that today the class will examine print research as evidence; during the next class, they will hear from a community leader or expert.

Analyzing Evidence (25 minutes)

- Explain that the class will be analyzing the evidence in an activity called a "jigsaw," where students first read a piece of evidence in small Learning Groups. The groups then split up and share what they learned with another group.

- Assemble the class into Learning Groups of 4–5 students and distribute the worksheets and 1 piece of evidence to each group. Tell the groups to begin reading the evidence and annotate the material by:

  - underlining what the evidence says is the problem;

  - circling anything the evidence says is a cause;

  - putting a star by the facts or information that the student thinks is most relevant to the class situation.

- *For middle school students:* Run through the exercise with 1 piece of information before sending them to work in small groups.

- Have students record their reactions to their material in the first column of the chart in the worksheet. Explain that, although they are working in their group, students should individually complete their own columns because they will next report about their evidence to other groups. Be sure to circulate around the room to help students with this task.

- After each group has individually completed their column, have the students in each group number off (1, 2, 3, 4, 5). Send students to their new groupings—the Expert Groups (all the 1s sit together, etc.)

- In these Expert Groups, have each student explain the materials he or she read in the Learning Groups. Students should take notes in the appropriate columns of their charts so they eventually have notes on every piece of evidence.

- After each Expert Group has heard the reports on the evidence, call on 1 student from each original Learning Group to explain in a few sentences the answers to the questions in the chart. Ask others to call out answers to help you fill in each column of the chart on the board.

Sample probing question

Where is the evidence in the article that shows that?

To enhance the discussion, use questions like

- Why might these have different views on cause?

- Who wrote these articles? How does their job/organization affect their views?

Discussing the Evidence (12 minutes)

- Initiate a whole-class discussion, asking students to compare and contrast the evidence using the following questions:
  - What do you notice is the same about the root cause across the difference pieces of evidence? What do you notice is different? Why is that?
  - Do you think that these root causes apply in our situation? Why or why not? If the evidence describes how the problem was solved in another situation, would that work here? Why or why not?
  - What do you still want to know more about? Where would we need more evidence to identify a root cause in *our* situation?

CONCLUSION (5 minutes)

- Preview the next class.
- Distribute the exit ticket. Ask a student to read the exit ticket prompt out loud or do this yourself.
- Instruct students to keep their worksheets in their In-Progress GC folder or submit them to you first for grading.
- Have students complete the exit ticket and submit it to you.

ASSESSMENT AND PORTFOLIO ELEMENTS

Exit Ticket: Examining Evidence

- Write down one fact you learned about root cause/our focus issue this class.
- Write down one question you still have about root cause/our focus issue.

COMMON CORE STANDARDS

- SL.8.2
- RH.6-8.3
- RH.6-8.4
- SL.9-10.2
- RH.9-10.3
- RH.9-10.4

Examining Evidence

DO-NOW

Word of the Day: _____

Definition: _____

_____

_____

_____

Sample Sentence: _____

_____

_____

_____

My Sentence: _____

_____

_____

_____

Favorite Pick: _____

_____

_____

_____

OVERVIEW AND OBJECTIVES

You will analyze evidence to determine the root cause of your focus problem. This examination will shape the class's goal and action plan.

By the end of this lesson, you will be able to:

- analyze research on the root cause of your focus issue;

- evaluate evidence about the root cause as it relates to the local context for your focus issue.

Learning Group Guidelines

In this group, your job is to learn as much as you can from the evidence you received. Follow the instructions below to read and mark key parts of your evidence. Take notes in the first column of the chart so that you have enough information to be an "expert" about this evidence in your second group.

As you read the evidence in your Learning Group:

- underline what the evidence says is the problem;

- circle anything the evidence says is a cause;

- put a star by the facts or information that you think is most interesting for our situation.

Expert Group Guidelines

In this group, your job is to share what you learned from the evidence in your Learning Group and to learn about the evidence that other groups have gathered. Take notes in the appropriate columns of the chart below so you have information from all the groups.

Title of Evidence:	Title of Evidence:	Title of Evidence:	Title of Evidence:
What does this article/evidence say is the problem?			
What information does the evidence use to prove this is a problem?			
According to the article/evidence, why is this problem happening?			
Compare/contrast this article to our school/neighborhood. What is different? What applies to our situation?			

EXIT TICKET

Examining Evidence

Instructions: Write your responses below. Hand this in to your teacher at the end of class.

1. Write down one fact you learned about root cause/our focus issue during this class.

_____

_____

_____

2. Write down one question you still have about root cause/our focus issue.

_____

_____

_____

COMMUNITY ISSUES

FOCUS ISSUE

ROOT CAUSE(S)

GOAL

TARGETS

TACTICS

Guest Speaker Invitation and Briefing Guide

Dear _____:

Our class has chosen to focus on the issue of _____ in [*name of community or school*]. Our first step in setting a class goal to help address this problem is to use evidence to find the root cause(s). This is where we could use your help. Might you visit our class to share your expertise about the issue?

In your visit, it would be especially valuable if you could speak about the following:

- Your personal and/or organization's experience with this issue in this particular community.

- Possible root cause(s) of this issue in this particular community:

  - Why do you think this problem exists in this community?

  - What do other people think causes this problem? Do you agree/disagree?

  - What is making the problem worse?

  - What is making the problem better?

  - What could make the problem worse?

  - What could make the problem better?

  - What evidence do you have for your answers above?

- Other information that might help us decide the root cause of this issue, including:

  - past actions that have worked in addressing this issue;

  - past actions that have not worked in addressing this issue;

  - affiliated important decision-makers;

  - possible allies for our class: who else in the community is working on this? How are they working on this? (funding/legislation/education);

  - possible adversaries: who in the community is against change on this issue and why?

We would like you to speak for about 20 minutes and then take questions from the class. Our class period lasts ___ minutes.

LESSON 5: FROM ROOT CAUSE TO GOAL

OVERVIEW

The class will analyze the issue to determine what possible root cause is most significant and which is most feasible to address. They will then draft a class goal for their project.

OBJECTIVES

By the end of this lesson, students will be able to:

- analyze and evaluate evidence provided by a guest speaker on the root cause of their focus issue;
- select a root cause by analyzing its importance and the feasibility of addressing it;
- create a goal that addresses the selected root cause.

WORD OF THE DAY

Feasible (adjective): Possible to do/accomplish; realistic

Sample Sentence: A lot of people thought going to the Moon would never be feasible—it was just something people dreamed of but it would never actually happen.

MATERIALS

- Worksheet: From Root Cause to Goal
- Exit Ticket: From Root Cause to Goal
- Unit 1 Assessment
- Unit 1 Assessment Rubric

PREPARATION BEFORE CLASS

- Be sure to confirm date, time, and place with the guest speaker and alert her to any potential check-in policies the school may have.

- *Optional:* If unable to bring in a speaker (or do a video chat), other options include:
  - examining more evidence;
  - having students conduct interviews with relevant community members out of class and then doing a jigsaw/small group to debrief the key points of the interviews.
- Prepare several possible goals for the action project aligned with the root cause identified in the class's research.
- Write the focus issue on the board (or reusable chart paper).
- Write Word of the Day and sample sentence on the board.
- Print a worksheet, an exit ticket, and a Unit 1 Assessment for each student.
- Post the Advocacy Hourglass if it is not already at the front of the class.

Note

It is very important that you prepare this lesson in advance if you invite a guest speaker.

To shorten this lesson

- Do today's exit ticket in another period or assign it for homework before the next class.
- If the class comes to consensus on the appropriate root cause quickly, you can shorten this lesson or combine it with the following one.

LESSON

Introduction (8 minutes)

- *Do-Now:*

  Word of the Day: Feasible
- *Lesson overview and framing:* Refer to the Advocacy Hourglass to show where the class is. Explain that today the class will finish determining the root cause of the focus issue and then use that analysis to set a goal. Remind students of norms for behavior when a speaker is visiting.

Hearing from an Expert (20–25 minutes)

- Distribute the worksheet. Tell students that as the speaker addresses them, they are to note what the speaker thinks the root cause is and what evidence she uses to support her position.
- Introduce the guest speaker. Have her present her thoughts about the root cause of the focus issue.
- Give the students a few minutes to ask questions.
- Thank the speaker and ensure that she knows how to exit the building.

Examining Options (10 minutes)

- Explain that the class will now select the cause they will focus on, which, in turn, will help them determine their goal for addressing the focus issue. By choosing 1 cause, they can concentrate their attention and be more effective. Explain that the Advocacy Hourglass narrows at this point so that both the cause and the goal are very specific.
- Draw the following T-chart on the board and have students add the causes they identified in Lesson 4 from their research and from their own knowledge. If you have invited a guest speaker, frame her presentation as another source of evidence that should be considered (and compared) alongside all the other research the class has done.

What do our experience and these sources say is the root cause of our focus issue? Why is this problem happening?	What evidence do we have that this is the root cause?

- As students offer suggestions, encourage them to be very specific in their language about the cause of the problem and its manifestation. To narrow options, you may also suggest combining similar ideas.

Note

While you should have completed extensive research in advance, if, during class, you find yourself unsure about any of the details of the research or root cause, acknowledge your uncertainty to the students and find the answer later. Issues are complicated, and you should give only accurate information, even if this involves additional research.

Probing questions to help students get specific in describing root cause

How would you describe the effects of the root cause? Who is affected by it? Let's get concrete. Give me an example.

Selecting Our Root Cause (15 minutes)

- Explain that the way to choose the root cause the class will focus on is to determine which of the suggested causes is the most important—and which is the most feasible for the class to address.

- Refer to the worksheet. Have students do a quick stop-and-jot. In a stop-and-jot, stop the conversation to have students independently and silently write their thoughts about the following:

  > Write down which 1–3 root causes from our T-chart are most important to you and what makes each of those important.

  > Use a timer or stopwatch to give students 2–5 minutes.

- Call on students to share their thoughts. As each student responds, put a check mark next to the root causes he identifies. (A cause may have multiple check marks.)

- Next, ask students to offer ideas about which of the causes that *already have a check mark by them* are also feasible for the class to tackle. Err on the side of presuming that the action will make a difference and encourage students in thinking expansively about possibilities. It is often possible to break down a complex cause into manageable pieces that could be tackled in a semester, yet still meaningfully contribute to solving the overall problem.

- Circle the causes that the students identify as feasible. *The cause with the most check marks and circles is the one the class should pick.* Rewrite this prominently on the board. Ask students to write the cause on their worksheets.

- If there is a tie, ask students which cause they are most excited to work on. You can acknowledge that many suggestions are valid but that they have to pick the most feasible so they can act in one semester.

Exemplar language for root cause

- Students are regularly getting mugged at the bus stop across the street from the school because police hardly ever patrol that area.
- Students have to pay for subway/bus passes because the city board of education has chosen not to fund reduced price or free passes.
- High school students who are pregnant/have kids are more likely to drop out because they have no child care options.

Non-exemplar language for root cause

- Students are getting mugged because of gangs.
- Subway/bus fares are too high because the public transit authority has to deal with budget cuts, so it has to raise fares.
- Students who are pregnant/have kids drop out because taking care of kids is a lot of work.

Probing questions to help guide students to prioritize

- Does anyone else agree with this? Did anyone else write down a root cause that we did not already mark?
- What evidence do you have that your cause is the most important?
- Referring back to the Word of the Day, "feasible," which characteristics of these options make them feasible?
- If students cannot agree on 1 cause, you may want to use some elements of the consensus-building process outlined in Lesson 3.

Drafting a Goal (12 minutes)

- Refer back to the Advocacy Hourglass and point out that the class will now turn their work on these previous steps into a goal. By having a clear goal, they will be able to determine what they need to do to make a sustainable change for their focus issue.
- Lead students in a discussion about the question: What is the effect or solution they want? Encourage them to consider how to ensure that their goal does not have a

short-term or one-time effect but addresses the problem long term or has meaningful systemic impact.

- With this desired impact and the identified root cause, write the following sentence stem on the board and lead students in completing this goal statement (see examples):

We will [*impact*]. By [*addressing root cause*], we will [*fix/deal with focus issue*].

Exemplar language for goal

- We will get the counseling office to create a mentoring program for 6th and 8th graders *(impact)*. By creating relationships between older and younger students *(addressing root cause)*, we will reduce bullying at our school *(fix/deal with focus issue)*.

- We will get the board of education to fund free/reduced price bus/subway passes for students living more than one mile from school *(impact)*. Having free/reduced price bus passes *(addressing root cause)* will make students less likely to be tardy or to miss school *(fix/deal with focus issue)*.

- We will get police to regularly patrol the bus stop across the street *(impact)*. By increasing the presence of police *(addressing root cause)*, we will reduce muggings at the bus stop *(fix/deal with focus issue)*.

Non-exemplar language for goal

- We will get students to care about and support ending bullying in the school.

- We will get the public transit authority to lower fares for the subway/bus.

- Our goal is to ensure that our community is a safe place to live.

Self-Check for the Specificity of the Goal

Could you easily determine a decision-maker from the way the class goal is worded?

CONCLUSION (5 minutes)

- Preview what students will be doing in the next class.
- Instruct students to keep their worksheets in their In-Progress GC folder or submit them to you first for grading.
- Distribute and review the Unit 1 Assessment. Remind students that this assessment will become part of their Portfolios.
- Distribute the exit ticket. Ask a student to read the exit ticket prompt out loud or do this yourself.

- Have students complete exit ticket and submit it to you.
- Follow up with the guest speaker by sending a thank you note or calling to express your thanks.

ASSESSMENT AND PORTFOLIO ELEMENTS

Exit Ticket: From Root Cause to Goal

Write down one-to-two actions we as a class could take to achieve our goal.

Portfolio: Unit 1 Assessment. Have the students complete the assessment outside of class and return it before Lesson 6.

Rubric: Unit 1 Assessment Rubric. Use this for grading/assessing Unit 1 Assessment before students place it in their Portfolio folder. You could distribute the rubrics to students to describe successful work.

COMMON CORE STANDARDS

- SL.8.6
- RH.6-8.3
- RH.6-8.4
- SL.9-10.6
- RH.9-10.3
- RH.9-10.4

WORKSHEET

From Root Cause to Goal

DO-NOW

Word of the Day: _____

Definition: _____

_____

_____

_____

Sample Sentence: _____

_____

_____

_____

My Sentence: _____

_____

_____

_____

Favorite Pick: _____

_____

_____

_____

OVERVIEW AND OBJECTIVES

By the end of this lesson, you will be able to:

- analyze and evaluate evidence provided by a guest speaker on the root cause of your focus issue;

- select a root cause by analyzing its importance and feasibility;

- create a goal that addresses an identified root cause.

ACTIVITY

Part 1: Hearing from an Expert

Instructions: Note what the speaker thinks the root cause is and what evidence he or she uses to support his or her position.

Name of Guest Speaker:

What does the speaker say is the root cause of our focus issue? Why is this problem happening?	What evidence does the speaker provide about why that is the root cause?

Part 2: Selecting Our Root Cause

Stop-and-jot: Which one-to-three root causes on the T-chart are most important to you, and what makes each of those important?

1. _____

    _____

2. _____

    _____

3. _____

    _____

Root cause we chose as a class:

_____

Goal: We will [*fill in our impact*]. By [*fill in how we address our root cause*], we will [*fill in our focus issue and how we fix it/deal with it*].

_____

_____

EXIT TICKET

From Root Cause to Goal

Instructions: Write your response below. Hand this in to your teacher at the end of class.

Write down one or two actions the class could take to achieve our goal.

1. _____

   _____

2. _____

   _____

Unit 1 Assessment

WHAT HAVE YOU LEARNED IN GENERATION CITIZEN SO FAR?

Instructions:

1. Read the story about a community issue and then fill in the community issues, focus issue, root cause, and goal in the Advocacy Hourglass. Label the sections of the Advocacy Hourglass. Use examples from the story to fill it in and make sure the parts of your Advocacy Hourglass connect. You may use your worksheets and notes that you took during class.

Story of Action

A group of 9th-grade students in Mr. Blanco's class were worried about some problems in their local community. Mr. Blanco's class saw that a lot of 9th graders were not going to classes or were quiet and not participating in class. They also saw that some of the 9th graders in their school were getting bullied in the hallways by some 10th and 11th graders between classes when no teachers were around. Mr. Blanco's class knew that the student council was respected by the whole school but 9th graders were not allowed on the council. The class knew that the student council was responsible for hosting a lot of school spirit activities and assemblies during the year. They also found out that the principal and the guidance counselor were responsible for running the student council.

2. On the back of your Advocacy Hourglass or on another sheet of paper, answer the following question(s). Explain your choices carefully.

   • Why did you choose this particular issue, root cause, and goal?

   For high school students:
   • Were there other options you could have chosen? Why are the answers you chose the most important ones?

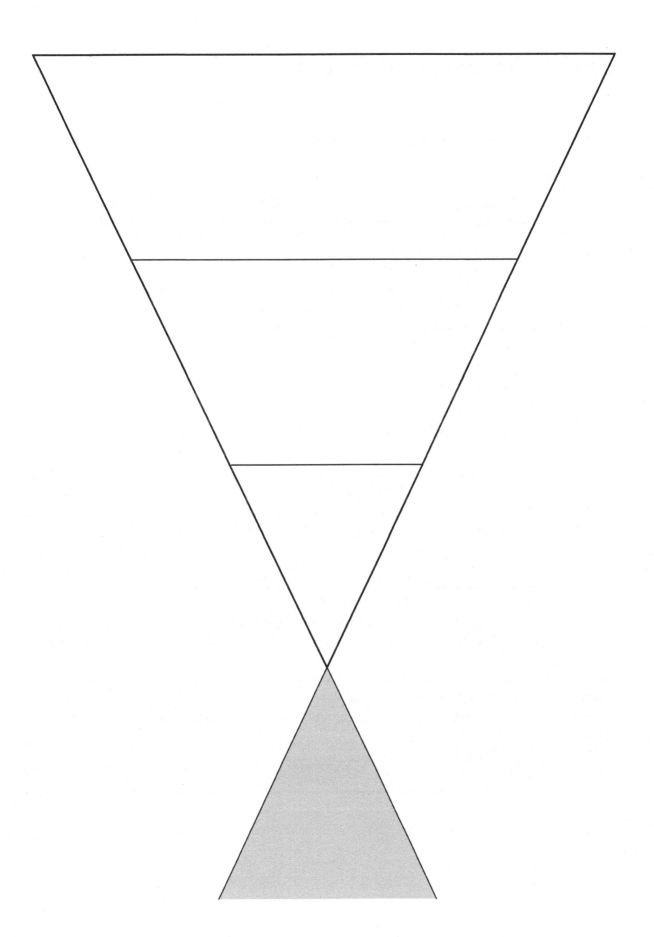

Unit 1 Assessment Rubric

Use this rubric to help you review your own work and as a checklist to make sure that you are including all required elements.

	Outstanding/ Exemplary	Proficient	Emerging/ Developing	Minimal/ Limited
Diagram	Chosen issues, causes, and goals demonstrate a deep understanding of the action process. They are interconnected and flow together. They offer a creative view of the community action.	Chosen issues, causes, and/or goals are logical and interrelated.	Chosen issues, causes, and/or goals are questionable. They are peripherally related.	Chosen issues, causes, and/or goals do not make sense. There is a lack of basic understanding of the process.
	Hourglass contains extensive details and examples from the story.	Hourglass includes some details and examples.	Hourglass includes very few examples and details.	Hourglass does not include details and examples.
	Note: Students can only get "proficient" in this area.	All sections of the hourglass are labeled correctly.	Some sections of the hourglass are labeled correctly.	No sections of the hourglass are labeled correctly.
Short Answer Question	Short answer question uses extensive evidence from the story.	Uses some evidence from the story.	Uses very minimal examples from the story.	Does not include evidence from the story.

	Clearly explains and analyzes the chosen issue, causes, and goals. Draws conclusions about why this option is arguably the most effective.	Clearly explains and analyzes the chosen issue, causes, and goals.	Mentions chosen issue, causes, and goals with little explanation.	Does not explain the reasons for the chosen issue, causes, and goals.
	Explains and analyzes issues, alternative causes, and goals. Draws conclusions about why these alternatives are not the most effective.	Discusses alternative issues, causes, and goals but does not analyze them.	Identifies alternative issues, causes, and goals, but does not discuss and analyze them.	Does not mention alternative issues, causes, and goals.
Overall	**If the student had an opportunity to edit:** No spelling and/or grammatical errors. Work is neat and organized.	**If the student had an opportunity to edit:** Minimal spelling and/or grammatical errors. Work is neat and organized.	**If the student had an opportunity to edit:** Errors of spelling or grammar and/or sloppy work make paper difficult to read.	**If the student had an opportunity to edit:** Errors of spelling or grammar and/or sloppy work prevent communication of ideas.

Comments/Grade:

UNIT 2: PLANNING OUR ACTION

MAIN GOALS

At the end of Unit 2, students will be able to:

- identify a decision-maker who can help them achieve their goal;
- analyze the decision-maker's role and responsibilities to create an "Ask" (a request);
- analyze the decision-maker's motivations and interests to draft arguments ("key messages") in support of the request;
- analyze key messages to determine "influencers" (potential supporters who could advocate for the goal);
- analyze a decision-maker's "pressure points" to identify targeted influencers;
- describe a variety of advocacy tactics;
- analyze their target audience to select tactics for their action plan.

Students will have:

- identified a decision-maker for their goal;
- created an "Ask" and set of key messages to persuade the decision-maker;
- identified and selected other targeted influencers who can help them achieve their goal by influencing the decision-maker;
- selected a set of tactics that will help them effectively reach and persuade their targets.

UNIT SUMMARY

Students now move into the planning process in earnest, selecting targets for their action. In Lesson 6, they use their goal statement to identify a decision-maker—a specific individual or member of a group who could effect the desired change. Students then look at the specific powers that the decision-maker has and draft an "Ask" they will make of the individual or group. They then analyze the decision-maker's own priority issues and responsibilities to craft key messages and arguments in support of their goal. Students turn to other targets in Lesson 7, considering individuals whose help they can enlist to influence the decision-maker. In Lesson 8, students determine how they will reach these targets, examining and choosing from an array of tactics, from writing op-eds to lobbying to holding a public meeting. After this lesson, the class is ready to break into project teams oriented toward the target decision-maker and influencers to begin executing their chosen tactics.

LESSON 6: IDENTIFYING A DECISION-MAKER

OVERVIEW

Students will analyze who has power to influence their issue, identify and select a decision-maker, draft an "Ask" of that decision-maker that will meet their goal, and analyze evidence or information about the decision-maker's possible motivations. Ultimately, they will create arguments explaining how the project's goal can serve the interests of both the class and the decision-maker.

Note

For some focus issues, such as school-related concerns, students will be able to identify a decision-maker relatively easily by class brainstorming. However, if addressing their focus issue involves city or state agencies, students may lack the knowledge to make such a determination. In these cases, you may need to bring in materials to help students identify and learn more about an individual decision-maker within a legislative/rule-making body. If this is the case, follow the procedure for analyzing evidence described in Lesson 4. The lesson below assumes that students have the requisite knowledge to identify a decision-maker. If this is not the case, class time may need to be adjusted accordingly.

OBJECTIVES

By the end of this lesson, students will be able to:

- identify a decision-maker who can help them achieve their goal;
- analyze the decision-maker's role and responsibilities to create an "Ask";
- analyze the decision-maker's motivations and interests in order to draft arguments ("key messengers") in support of their Ask.

WORD OF THE DAY

Influential (adjective): Having the power to produce effects on the behavior, actions, or opinions of others

Sample Sentence: Jeremy's basketball coach was very influential in his life: if his coach recommended changes to Jeremy's diet, exercises, or study schedule, Jeremy always made them.

MATERIALS

- Worksheet: Identifying a Decision-Maker
- Exit Ticket: Identifying a Decision-Maker
- Collected research on the Decision-Maker (see Preparation Before Class below)
- Chart paper

PREPARATION BEFORE CLASS

- Familiarize yourself with possible key decision-maker(s) who can help the class achieve their goal.

Sample Decision-Makers

- Business owners/members of business organizations
- Clergy/religious leaders
- Elected officials
- Faculty and administrators at local colleges
- Media personalities
- Opinion leaders
- Members of organizations that represent voters (e.g., NAACP, unions)
- Members of organizations that helped elect the decision-maker
- Parents
- People directly affected by the issue you're working on
- Teachers
- Other leaders of community organizations

- Find two types of information on these decision-makers:

  1. Information about the roles and power of this decision-maker:
     - What is her job?
     - What does she have power/control over?
     - How does she exercise that power? (Write a proposal? Design a budget? Approve a policy? Hire someone?)

  2. Information about the decision-maker's motivations to shed light on the following questions:
     - What are the biggest issues the decision-maker is facing now? What issues has she been working on recently?
     - What does her job description make her care about? What is she responsible for? Who is she accountable to?

Note

This decision-maker research could include formal job descriptions, current news reports related to her, etc. For an in-school issue, you might just need to share information with the class. We recommend that you offer your students this material to review during the discussion to better guide their responses.

- Print a worksheet and exit ticket for each student.
- Write the class goal on the board to focus the day's conversation.
- Write the Word of the Day and sample sentence on the board.
- Post the Advocacy Hourglass if it is not already at the front of the class.
- Reproduce the following chart on the chart paper. (You will need the chart for future lessons.)

Name:

Ask:

Pressure Points	Key Messages

To shorten this lesson

Do today's exit ticket in another period or assign it for homework to be completed before the next class.

To enhance this lesson

You can bring in a case study from the local news to offer students an opportunity to practice identifying the key decision-maker and influencers before working on their own issue.

LESSON

Introduction (8 minutes)

- *Do-Now:*

  Word of the Day: Influential

- *Lesson overview and framing:* Review the Advocacy Hourglass process to show students that they are now building their plan to reach their goal. Explain that to identify their targets and decide on a course of action, they need to determine who has the power to help them achieve their objective. This person, the decision-maker, will become their most important target. Emphasize that everything they do from now on will be designed to get a decision-maker to do what they want her to do to accomplish the goal.

Identifying a Decision-Maker (20 minutes)

- Introduce the 2 types of people the class will be considering in their plan.
  - *Decision-maker:* The person or body whose decision alone could achieve the result they want.
  - *Other Influencers:* People or groups who can help us because they have influence with the decision-maker.
- Explain that the students will learn more about Influencers in the next lesson,
- Explain that there is not always just one decision-maker who could help the class achieve their goal, but that they will pick just one individual (who may be a member of a larger decision-making body, like a city council or school board) and focus their efforts on that person—at least to start. (If the problem can be solved only by a larger body, eventually they may have to approach more than one individual.) Lead this discussion by asking:

  Thinking about our goal and the root cause(s) we've determined, who has the power to directly solve our problem?

  Write the suggestions on the board.
- Ask students which person on this list must we convince if we are to achieve our goal?

  Guide students in answering the above question by reviewing the materials you have collected or using their own knowledge of local or school-based issues.
- Once the students have determined who will be their decision-maker, distribute the worksheet and ask them to record this person's name in the first line of the chart. Do the same on the master chart.
- Ask students to do a quick stop-and-jot responding to the following question:

Why do we think this person is the decision-maker we must influence/convince to achieve our goal? (e.g., Why ask the precinct captain to address the problem of muggings on the corner? Because he controls where officers are stationed.)

Analyzing Our Decision-Maker (17 minutes)

- Explain that now that the class has identified a decision-maker, they need to think about what matters to him so that they can create a plan to convince him to do what they ask. The class must put themselves in his shoes.

- Explain that the class's first task is to develop an "Ask" for the decision-maker based on the goal. Explain that an Ask clearly states what the students want the decision-maker to do. Distribute the information you've gathered or use student-based knowledge to discuss the following questions. Note their ideas on the chart paper.

  - What is the decision-maker's job?

  - What does he have power or control over?

  - How does he exercise that power? (Design a budget? Approve a policy? Hire someone?)

- At the end of the discussion, write the following sentence stem on the board and have the students complete the Ask.

  We want [*the decision-maker*] to [*exercise what power*] to [*accomplish what*].

  Tell them to add the Ask to their charts; add the Ask to the class chart.

- Explain that now that the class has an Ask, they need to consider what will make the decision-maker want to help them. These motivations we call "pressure points." Using the information you gathered, lead a discussion to guide students to answer the following questions:

  - What are the biggest issues the decision-maker is facing right now? What issues has she been working on recently?

  - What does her job description make her care about? What is she responsible for? To whom is she accountable?

- As the class determines these pressure points, have students write them in the appropriate column of the chart in the worksheet and on the class chart.

- Finally, explain that the class now has everything they need to develop key messages—arguments that will convince the decision-maker to help them achieve their goal. An effective way to get someone to do what you want is to frame the goal as mutually beneficial. A key message is a statement about the connection between the class's goal and the decision-maker's interests.

- Have students complete a stop-and-jot that offers suggestions for key messages to answer the following question:

  How can [*doing our Ask*] help the decision-maker address his or her concern about his or her [*pressure point/issue*]?

The answers to this question will become the key messages—in other words, *what* the class will say to convince the decision-maker. The format for the key messages is:

By [*fulfilling our Ask*], [*decision-maker*] can both [*address our goal*] and [*address decision-maker's pressure point*].

Write these key messages on the chart and have students write them on their worksheets.

- Save the completed chart. You will need it for the following lessons.

Exemplar "Ask" language

- To a principal: create a mentoring program for 6th and 8th graders that starts at the beginning of the school year and continues at least once per month.

- To a member of the board of education: introduce and pass a proposal to fund free/reduced price bus/subway passes for students living more than one mile from school at the next board meeting.

- To a police precinct captain: deploy police officers in the area around the bus stop and patrol the area—especially when students are leaving school in the afternoon/ early evening.

Non-exemplar "Ask" language

- To a principal: make an announcement saying you support ending bullying at our school.

- To a member of the board of education: support lowering subway/bus fares.

- To a police precinct captain: stop muggings in our area.

Exemplar pressure point language

- To a principal: responsible for students' safety and discipline in the school building. If a principal has to make too many suspensions, the school may be labeled a "persistently dangerous school," which has a number of negative consequences.

- To a member of the board of education: elected directly by voters or appointed by a mayor (who is, in turn, elected by voters). Responsible for policies to ensure students receive a quality education in an entire school district/city. Bad results from schools they oversee and/or bad press can jeopardize their reelection/reappointment. Much of their budget may need to be provided by the city council or state legislature, so they must maintain good relationships with those officials.

- To a police precinct captain: reports to police commissioner, who oversees police department, appointed directly by a mayor (who is, in turn, elected by voters). Precinct captain is responsible for public safety in a given geographic area. Higher crime rates can jeopardize their job prospects. Reducing crime often depends on the trust and close cooperation of the neighborhood and its residents.

Non-exemplar pressure point language

- To a principal: principals should care about students, so if s/he's not doing what we want, that's a problem.
- To a member of the board of education: they get elected by our parents/appointed by the mayor (who is, in turn, elected by our parents), so they need to do what we want.
- To a police precinct captain: they get promoted or demoted by the police commissioner, who's appointed by the mayor our parents elected, so s/he needs to do what we say.

Exemplar key message language

- To a principal: By creating a mentoring program for 6th and 8th graders, our principal can both prevent bullying and give our school the reputation for safety and excellence that it deserves.
- To a member of the board of education: By funding public transportation for students who live more than a mile away from school, the board of education can reduce student tardiness and absenteeism, which increase the dropout rate and, by reducing the average daily attendance, jeopardize school funding.
- To a police precinct captain: By deploying officers near the bus stop and school, especially in the afternoons/early evenings, the precinct captain can reduce crime in our area and increase community support for the police department.

Non-exemplar key message language

- Our principal needs to create a mentoring program or he will lose his job because we'll be rated a persistently dangerous school.
- Students hate having to walk three miles in the cold, and parents can't afford subway/bus passes on their own, so funding free/reduced price passes is the right thing to do
- The precinct captain needs to stop muggings in our area because otherwise the police commissioner will fire or demote him/her.

CONCLUSION (5 minutes)

- Preview what students will be doing in the next class.
- Distribute the exit ticket. Call on a student to read the exit ticket prompt out loud or do this yourself.
- Instruct students to keep their worksheets in their In-Progress GC folder or submit them to you first for grading.
- Have students complete exit ticket and submit it to you.

ASSESSMENT AND PORTFOLIO ELEMENTS

Exit Ticket: Identifying a Decision-Maker

If you could meet with our decision-maker and tell him or her three things that would make him or her support our goal, what would those be? Use three complete sentences.

1.

2.

3.

COMMON CORE STANDARDS

- SL.8.2
- WHST.6-8.7
- SL.9-10.2
- WHST.9-10.7

WORKSHEET

Identifying a Decision-Maker

DO-NOW

Word of the Day: _____

Definition: _____

_____

_____

_____

Sample Sentence: _____

_____

_____

_____

My Sentence: _____

_____

_____

_____

Favorite Pick: _____

_____

_____

_____

OVERVIEW AND OBJECTIVES

You will analyze who has direct power to solve the problem created by your focus issue, identify and select a decision-maker, and draft an Ask—a request of the decision-maker that will help meet our goal—and analyze evidence or information about the decision-maker's motivations. This will lead to the creation of key messages explaining how the project's goal can serve the interests of both the class and the decision-maker.

By the end of this lesson, you will be able to:

- identify a decision-maker who can help us achieve our goal;
- analyze the decision-maker's role and responsibilities to create an Ask;
- analyze the decision-maker's motivations and interests to draft key messages.

ACTIVITY

1. Fill out the top line of the chart below with the name of the decision-maker.

2. Do a stop-and-jot answering the following question:

    Why do we think this person is the decision-maker we need to influence to achieve our goal?

    _____

    _____

3. Complete the Ask and add it to the chart. Remember to formulate the Ask as follows:

    We want [*the decision-maker*] to [*exercise what power*] to [*accomplish what*].

4. Fill in at least one pressure point for the decision-maker.

5. Complete a stop-and-jot, offering suggestions for key messages to answer the following question:

    How can doing our "Ask" help the decision-maker address his or her concerns about his or her pressure points or issues?

    _____

    _____

6. Write at least one key message that you will use to convince the decision-maker to do what you ask. Formulate the key message as follows:

By [*fulfilling our Ask*], [*decision-maker*] can both [*address our goal*] and [*address decision-maker's pressure point*].

Add this to the chart.

Analyzing the Decision-Maker

Name:

Ask:

Pressure Points	Key Messages

EXIT TICKET

Identifying a Decision-Maker

Instructions: Answer the question below and hand this to your teacher as you leave.

If you could meet with our decision-maker and tell him or her three facts that would make him or her more likely to support our goal, what would those be? Use three complete sentences.

1. _____

   _____

2. _____

   _____

3. _____

   _____

LESSON 7: TARGETING INFLUENCERS

OVERVIEW

Students will review the decision-maker and key messages to identify other targets who could be "influencers" on this issue, and who could be brought together to form a coalition in support of their goal. Students then rank those targets based on their potential influence on the decision-maker. With these targeted influencers in mind, students will then be ready to learn about and select tactics.

OBJECTIVES

By the end of this lesson, students will be able to:

- analyze key messages to determine potential supporters ("influencers");
- analyze a decision-maker's "pressure points" to identify targeted influencers.

WORD OF THE DAY

Coalition (noun): A group of people/smaller groups working together for a common goal

Sample Sentence: The Civil Rights Movement successfully created a coalition of African Americans and antisegregation whites to push for equality.

MATERIALS

- Worksheet: Targeting Influencers
- Exit Ticket: Targeting Influencers
- Any needed outside research (see below for specifics)

PREPARATION BEFORE CLASS

- Familiarize yourself with potential allies who could influence the decision-maker and thus help achieve the goal.

- Determine what type of research you might need (if any) to guide your students in identifying what motivates the allies they brainstorm. You may need outside research, a guest speaker from within the school, etc. (See Lesson 4 for ways to help students analyze this research.)
- Post the Advocacy Hourglass and Analyzing the Decision-Maker chart from Lesson 6 on the board.
- Write the Word of the Day and sample sentence on the board.

To shorten this lesson

Do today's exit ticket in another period or assign it as homework to be completed before the next class.

LESSON

Introduction (8 minutes)

- *Do-Now:*

  Word of the Day: Coalition

- *Lesson overview and framing:* Refer to the Advocacy Hourglass. Explain that while identifying and convincing a decision-maker is essential, if the class relies solely on one person to help them, they're unlikely to be successful if the decision-maker doesn't agree to do what they want. Therefore, the class will have to determine who else can influence the decision-maker and target those individuals as well. Sometimes, you can organize influencers into a coalition, which can help amplify your voice. (Not all influencers will necessarily join a given coalition, though.) To start targeting influencers, the class needs to review what they did in Lesson 6.

Reviewing Key Messages (17 minutes)

- Review the Analyzing the Decision-Maker chart from Lesson 6 by calling on different students to explain in their own words what the elements of the chart mean.
- Break the class into small groups, distribute the worksheet, and assign one of the key messages from Lesson 6's chart to each group. (Alternatively, have the entire class do a stop-and-jot to consider ideas and then discuss as a whole class.)
- Have the groups brainstorm 2–3 potential influencers who might respond to their key message using the following question:

  Who already cares the most about this issue and this message?

- After several minutes, have students reassemble as a class to share their ideas. Write each group's suggestions on the board and discuss. You may need to use your research to supplement students' knowledge of each potential influencer.

Analyzing Influencers (20 minutes)

- Explain that the class must next determine which influencers are most worthy of their attention, based on 2 criteria: 1) who has the most influence on our decision-maker and 2) who can the class influence most. To do this, they will plot the names on a Venn diagram. Those who fall in the middle will be the main targets of our work.

- Draw a Venn diagram on the board like the one below and explain how Venn diagrams work.

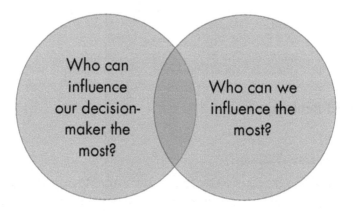

- Call on students to give you suggestions on where to place each individual on the diagram. Lead the conversation using the following questions:
  - For "Who can influence our decision-maker?"
    - Which pressure points does this influencer connect with?
    - What kinds of people does our decision-maker listen to or care about?
  - For "Whom can we influence the most?" (Err on the side of encouraging students to believe they can influence an individual.)
    - Who is easily accessible? Who do we have personal connections to?
    - Who would care about students and therefore be an easy target?
- Use the Venn diagram and class discussion to narrow the list to 2–3 influencers for the entire class. Write these names on the board and on the Advocacy Hourglass.
- Tell the students to think about how the influencer can get the decision-maker to do what the class wants. Call on students to help the class complete the following sentence stem describing their Ask for each selected influencer:

    Because [*name and title of influencer*] cares about [*issue/message*] and has influence on [*decision-maker*], we will ask him or her to [*Ask of influencer*].

CONCLUSION (5 minutes)

- Preview what the students will be doing in the next class.
- Distribute the exit ticket. Call on a student to read the prompt out loud or do this yourself.
- Instruct students to keep their worksheets in their In-Progress GC folder or submit them to you first for grading.
- Have students complete the exit ticket and submit it to you.

ASSESSMENT AND PORTFOLIO ELEMENTS

Exit Ticket: Targeting Influencers

Pick a target (a decision-maker or influencer) who you would be particularly interested in focusing on. Think carefully because this may help your teacher determine which project team would best fit you. Write two-to-three sentences about why you think that target would be important and exciting.

COMMON CORE STANDARDS

- SL.8.2
- SL.8.4
- RH.6-8.6
- RH.6-8.7
- WHST.6-8.9
- SL.9-10.2
- SL.9-10.4

- RH.9-10.6
- RH.9-10.7
- WHST.9-10.9

WORKSHEET

Targeting Influencers

DO-NOW

Word of the Day: _____

Definition: _____

_____

_____

_____

Sample Sentence: _____

_____

_____

_____

My Sentence: _____

_____

_____

_____

Favorite Pick: _____

_____

_____

_____

OVERVIEW AND OBJECTIVES

You will review the decision-maker and key messages to identify other persons who could be influencers on this issue (some of whom you might organize as a coalition). You then rank those individuals based on their potential influence on the decision-maker.

By the end of this lesson, you will be able to:

• analyze key messages to determine potential supporters;

• analyze a decision-maker's "pressure points" to identify targeted influencers.

ACTIVITY

Part 1. Reviewing Key Messages

Write the key message assigned to your group in the first row and then brainstorm two or three possible influencers. Write their names in the second row. Think about: Who already cares the most about this issue and this message? Share your ideas with the class.

Key Message:
Possible Influencers:
1.
2.
3.

Part 2. Analyzing Influencers

Write the names of the two or three influencers the class has decided to target in the table below. Then write down the class's Ask for each.

Influencer	Ask

EXIT TICKET

Targeting Influencers

Instructions: Write your response below and hand the completed sheet to your teacher at the end of class.

Pick a target (a decision-maker or influencer) who you would be particularly interested in focusing on. Think carefully because this may help your teacher determine which project team would best fit you. Write two-to-three sentences about why you think that target would be important and exciting.

_____

_____

_____

_____

_____

LESSON 8: SELECTING TACTICS

OVERVIEW

Students will review different types of advocacy tactics and analyze which actions might be most effective in influencing the decision-maker and influencers they have identified in the previous lessons. These tactics will form the basic content of the work that the project teams will do in Unit 3.

Note

Exit ticket *must* be completed today.

After this lesson, students will need to complete the Unit 2 Assessment outside of GC class and should return the assignment before the following lesson.

OBJECTIVES

By the end of this lesson, students will be able to:

- describe a variety of advocacy tactics;
- analyze their target audience to select tactics for the final stage of their Advocacy Hourglass plan.

WORD OF THE DAY

Benefit (verb): To get an advantage or some type of good out something/someone

Sample Sentence: Both cities benefited when the bridge connecting them was finished.

MATERIALS

- Worksheet: Selecting Tactics
- Exit Ticket: Selecting Tactics
- Unit 2 Assessment
- Unit 2 Assessment Rubric

PREPARATION BEFORE CLASS

- Familiarize yourself with each of the tactics in the worksheet.
- Print a worksheet, exit ticket, and assessment materials for each student.
- Write the Word of the Day and sample sentence on the board.
- Draw the following table on the board and write the information the class built over Lessons 6 and 7 in the first three columns of the table. Add or subtract rows depending on the number of people the class will be targeting.

Targets and Tactics

Person	Key Message	Ask	Tactics
Decision-maker			1. 2. 3.
Influencer (name):			1. 2. 3.
Influencer (name):			1. 2. 3.
Influencer (name):			1. 2. 3.

LESSON

Introduction (8 minutes)

- *Do-Now:*

    Word of the Day: Benefit

- *Lesson overview and framing:* Explain that students can use various tactics to get their message across to the decision-maker and influencers. The class will be spending the rest of the semester working in teams using these tactics, so choosing those that will be most effective is important.

Examining Tactics (18 minutes)

- Remind students that tactics are the actions we take to convey our messages. Distribute the worksheet and briefly review the tactics listed.

- Explain that students will now think about which tactics would best convince these targets—and therefore achieve the class's goal.

- Organize the students into 8 groups (one for each tactic listed on the worksheet) and assign a tactic to each. In their groups, have students complete the Tactic Table on their worksheet.

- After they have completed their table, have each group give a 30-second description of their tactic.

Picking Our Tactics (19 minutes)

- Lead a whole-class discussion about which tactics should be included in the Targets and Tactics Table to influence the different individuals in the first column. You may use questions such as:

  - What are the ways this person hears about issues?

  - Based on what we know about the decision-maker or influencers' pressure points, what kind of action might be most persuasive? (public, direct, group, individual, etc.)

  - Which tactics seems to "fit" best to convey our particular messages? (e.g., Message = lots of your constituents care about this; Possible Tactics = surveys, highly attended public meeting)

    Have students simultaneously complete their own version of this table on their worksheet.

    By the end of the conversation, the class should have created 1–3 tactics for each individual listed in the table.

- Have students complete the following prompt:

    Pick one target in the Targets and Tactics Table. Explain in two sentences (in your own words) why the tactics we picked will convince this person to do what we need.

Sample probing questions to drive student conversation on tactics

- What tactics are connected and might need to be used in conjunction with one another? (e.g., calls and emails to set up a meeting to build a coalition.)

- Which targets might be persuaded through the same type of tactic? How can we collaborate in our teams to take advantage of that?

CONCLUSION (5 minutes)

- Preview what they will be doing in the next class.
- Distribute the exit ticket. Call on a student to read the assignment out loud or do this yourself.
- Instruct students to keep their worksheets in their In-Progress GC folder or submit them to you first for grading.
- Distribute and review the Unit 2 Assessment. Remind them that this assessment will become part of their Portfolios.
- Have students complete the exit ticket and submit it to you.

ASSESSMENT AND PORTFOLIO ELEMENTS

Exit Ticket: Selecting Tactics

Which decision-makers or influencer(s) would you be most excited to use these tactics on and why?

Portfolio: Unit 2 Assessment. Have students complete the assessment independently outside of class and return it before Lesson 9.

Rubric: Unit 2 Assessment Rubric. Use this for grading/assessing the Unit 2 Assessment before placing it in the student Portfolios. You could distribute the rubrics to students to describe successful work.

COMMON CORE STANDARDS

- SL.8.1
- SL.8.4
- RH.6-8.4
- WHST.8.1
- SL.9-10.1
- SL.9-10.4
- RH.9-10.4
- WHST.9-10.1

WORKSHEET

Selecting Tactics

DO-NOW

Word of the Day: _____

Definition: _____

_____

_____

_____

Sample Sentence: _____

_____

_____

_____

My Sentence: _____

_____

_____

_____

Favorite Pick: _____

_____

_____

_____

OVERVIEW AND OBJECTIVES

You will review different types of advocacy tactics and analyze which actions might be most effective to influence the key decision-maker and influencers you identified in the previous lessons. These tactics will form the basic content of the work project teams will do in Unit 3.

By the end of this lesson, you will be able to:

- describe a variety of advocacy tactics;

- analyze your target audience to select tactics for the final stage of your Advocacy Hourglass plan.

Tactics

- **Lobbying.** The action of trying to convince, or persuade, another person of something. In relation to your project, you will need to persuade a decision-maker to take an action that will help you accomplish your goal.

- **Letters, emails, and calls.** Hearing from constituents, or the people for whom they are responsible, helps decision-makers take a position on an issue and prioritize which issues they will spend their time and energy on. An effective way for you and your coalition members to make your voices heard is to directly send letters to, call, or email decision-makers.

- **Surveys.** Use these to gauge opinions on your issue. The results will help inform you about how you best to move forward.

- **Public meetings.** You can use these to educate, influence, and/or mobilize large numbers of people (decision-makers, coalition partners, the public), or even to generate media attention. A public meeting might come in the form of a town meeting, school assembly, panel discussion, or workshop—to name a few.

- **Coalition-building.** Forming a coalition can be a critical part of your action plan. Building coalitions demonstrates to decision-makers that key individuals or groups support your issue. To build a successful coalition, influential people and groups must be enlisted, or recruited/convinced/persuaded, to join the cause—the best way to do this is to have a face-to-face meeting. (Note, however, that not all influencers can or should be members of a coalition.)

- **Social media.** This tactic includes web-based and mobile technologies such as Facebook, Twitter, YouTube, blogs (online discussion or information sites where people/organizations write individual posts on certain issues), or anything that turns communication into an interactive experience between users. You can use social media to generate publicity for an event, raise awareness on an issue, and interact with supporters and keep them informed about your group and your issue.

- **"Op-ed."** This stands for "opposite the editorial page." Newspaper editors share their opinions on the editorial page. On the facing page, editors allow outside contributors to express their thoughts and opinions. Op-eds are opinion articles written by members of the public and, sometimes, regular columnists. Newspapers often publish op-eds whose authors are experts or authorities in their field.

- **Letters to the editor.** These brief letters give ordinary citizens the opportunity to express their personal opinion about articles in newspapers and magazines.

ACTIVITY

Examining Tactics

Instructions: Fill out the following chart based on the tactic assigned your group.

Tactic Table

Tactic:	
Describe this tactic in your own words	
What does this tactic do?	
Who would this influence? Who reads this, sees this, or participates?	

Picking Our Tactic

Instructions:

1. Fill in the first three columns using the information your teacher has written on the board. Then, after the class discussion, fill in the tactics your class chooses to actually reach the targets in your plan.

   You will use this chart as a reference for the rest of the term.

Target and Tactics Table

Target Person	Key Message	Ask	Tactic(s)
Decision-maker:			

2. Pick one target in the chart above. Explain in two sentences (in your own words) why the tactic(s) the class has chosen will convince this person to do what we are asking.

EXIT TICKET

Selecting Tactics

Instructions: Write your response below. Hand this in to your teacher at the end of class.

Which decision-makers or influencer(s) would you be most excited to use these tactics on and why?

_____

_____

_____

_____

_____

_____

COMMUNITY ISSUES

FOCUS ISSUE

ROOT CAUSE(S)

GOAL

TARGETS

TACTICS

Unit 2 Assessment

WHAT HAVE YOU LEARNED IN GENERATION CITIZEN SO FAR?

Instructions:

Please read the story about a community action and then fill in the Tactics Table. Include tactics that will be the most help in achieving the goal in this story. You should have at least four tactics designed to reach at least two individuals. You may use your worksheets and the notes that you took during class. Use another sheet of paper if you need more space.

To be successful you should use examples from the Story of Action, make sure your Asks and tactics work together toward the goal, and clearly explain your recommendations by answering the two questions below.

Story of Action

- **Situation:** At our high school, the student council is respected, has a lot of student leaders, and runs school spirit assemblies and events. No 9th-grade students are allowed to serve on the student council. The principal and the guidance counselor are responsible for running the student council.

- **Focus Issue:** Bullying of the 9th graders in our school

- **Root Cause:** 9th-grade students are new to the school and don't feel connected to older students who can give them advice or support.

- **Goal:** We will get 9th-grade positions added to the student council next year. By giving 9th graders a voice and connecting the 9th-grade class to older student leaders, we will prevent bullying of 9th graders in our school.

Tactics Table

Decision-maker or Influencer	Ask	Tactic(s)

1. Why did you pick the people you wrote in the first column above? Why are they the most important people to help achieve the goal?

2. Why did you choose these specific tactics? Explain how these tactics might work together to achieve the goal.

Unit 2 Assessment Rubric

Outstanding/ Exemplary	Proficient	Emerging/ Developing	Minimal/Limited
Tactics chosen demonstrate a deep understanding of the process. The tactics complement one another and are clearly related to an effort to reach the goal.	Tactics chosen demonstrate a logical process toward addressing root causes and reaching the goal.	Tactics are questionable. There is little logic in why they were chosen and no relationship between them.	Tactics do not make sense.
Chart contains extensive details and examples from the story.	Chart includes some details and examples.	Chart includes only a few examples and very few details.	Chart does not include details and examples.
Explanation uses extensive evidence from the story.	Explanation uses some evidence from the story.	Explanation has very minimal evidence from the story.	Does not include evidence from the story.
Answers clearly explain and analyze the chosen tactics. Draws conclusions about why these tactics are arguably the most effective.	Answers clearly explain and analyze the chosen tactics.	Answers mention chosen tactics with little explanation.	Answers do not explain the reasons for the chosen tactics.
If the student had an opportunity to edit: No spelling and/or grammatical errors. Work is neat and organized.	**If the student had an opportunity to edit:** Minimal spelling and/or grammatical errors. Work is neat and organized.	**If the student had an opportunity to edit:** Errors in spelling or grammar and/or sloppy work make paper difficult to read.	**If the student had an opportunity to edit:** Errors in spelling or grammar and/or sloppy work prevent communication of ideas.

Comments/Grade:

UNIT 3: TAKING ACTION

MAIN GOALS

At the end of Unit 3, students will be able to:

* work in teams to analyze their tactics, create work plans, and assign roles;
* plan and execute a range of tactics involving oral and written persuasive communication, critical thinking, and group collaboration;
* define, identify, and utilize the components of effective persuasion;
* design a persuasive argument for the decision-maker or an influencer;
* analyze an influencer's priorities and responsibilities in order to enlist her help.

Students will have:

* collaboratively designed a work plan to execute a tactic with their project team;
* undertaken and executed a tactic to help persuade a target and achieve their goal.

UNIT SUMMARY

After determining their tactics, students break into project teams to create work plans, assign roles to execute those tactics, and carry out their action plan. Teachers select mini-lessons on advocacy tactics as they become relevant. Students practice and employ persuasive writing and speaking, group collaboration, and research skills to achieve their goal.

LESSON 9: PROJECT TEAMS

OVERVIEW

In project teams organized around the decision-maker or influencer(s), students will begin planning the work they must do to actively use the tactics that contribute to the overall plan and goal of the project. They will also create specific work plans and assign roles within their groups to hold themselves accountable.

OBJECTIVES

By the end of this lesson, students will be able to:

- work in teams to analyze their tactics;
- create work plans and assign roles.

WORD OF THE DAY

Collaborate (verb): To cooperate/work together on an activity

Sample Sentence: By collaborating with other students and teachers, the class was able to convince the principal to create more after-school clubs.

MATERIALS

- Worksheet: Project Teams
- Tactic Toolkit
- Exit Ticket: Project Teams

PREPARATION BEFORE CLASS

- Determine how many teams would work best for your classroom, how you will manage and interact with them, and how many targets (decision-maker and/or influencers) each team will be responsible for. Teams usually average 4–5 students, but numbers are flexible. We recommend that each team focus on no more than 2 people.

- Decide whether you will institute a student leadership team in the class who will act as liaisons between groups rather than focusing on the decision-maker or influencers.
- Use the exit tickets from Lesson 8 to create an initial plan for dividing the class into groups.
- Determine any contingency for rearranging groups based on student input.
- Write the Word of the Day and sample sentence on the board.
- Print the Tactic Toolkit for each student.
- Print a worksheet and exit ticket for each student.
- *For middle school students*: prepare simple work plan suggestions for actions, time lines, and roles.

Note

If large-scale printing/copying is an issue, you may distribute only those specific Tactic Toolkit sections each group will use. However, we recommend providing the entire Toolkit as a resource students can use during the course and for future advocacy.

To shorten this lesson

Have students complete the final 2 rows of the work plan for homework.

LESSON

Introduction (8 minutes)

- *Do-Now:*

    Word of the Day: Collaborate

- *Lesson overview and framing:* Explain that, for the rest of the term, students will work in teams to implement their advocacy plan. Each team will be organized around 1 or 2 targets—the decision-maker and/or influencers— and will work on implementing the tactics chosen to persuade those individuals. The first job of each team is to develop a work plan that will ensure that the class can reach their goal by the end of the term and that each member of the team knows his or her responsibilities in the group effort.

- Explain that working in teams is particularly beneficial in achieving the goal because each group is able to concentrate their efforts on 1 or 2 individuals. Actual advocacy campaigns work the same way. Explain that after students develop their plans, they will use different materials to learn more, practice, and implement their tactics.

Breaking into Teams (5 minutes)

- Explain that you used the exit tickets from Lesson 8 to assign students to teams. Not everyone got their first choice of team, but everyone will help decide her or his individual contributions to the team and to the whole class.

- *Optional if your class will have a leadership team:* If you decide to use a leadership team, assign students this role and have them focus their work plan on how they will check in with and ensure collaboration between the teams during class.

- Have students move into their assigned teams.

Discuss Collaboration (5 minutes)

- Explain that although each team will function independently, collaboration between the teams is the only way that the class can accomplish their goal.

- Have students complete a stop-and-jot on a separate piece of paper to answer the question:

    Why is communication and cooperation among groups important to achieve our goal?

Creating Work Plans (27 minutes)

- Once the students are in small groups, distribute the worksheets and have the students refer to them to develop their work plan. They should begin by transferring the name of the individual on which they will focus and the tactics the class has determined to reach that individual to the top of their sheet. If they are to concentrate on more than one individual, they should create a separate sheet for each. Remind students that although they are working as a group, they should fill in the group's answers on their own worksheet.

- Direct students to the Tactic Tool materials pages for the tactics in their plan if they need ideas for a preview of steps they will need to take.

- Explain that groups will use this work plan as a guide for what they will need to do. Sometimes, the members of the group may work independently, so the group must have a strong work plan to keep everyone on track. They will use the Tactic Toolkit to learn about and practice the specific tactics they will use. Not every group will use every part of the Toolkit; rather, each group will become experts in the particular tactics for which they are responsible.

- (If time) Ask the groups to start reading in-depth about one of the tactics they will be using. Have them ask questions or comment on what they read. They may also start on initial activities.

Note

Middle school students may need more prescriptive guidance in this process, so be prepared to help them set realistic plans and a time line. You may also need to present middle school students with specific options for roles and responsibilities within the team based on your preparations. You may want to discuss the process as a class and use the board to model some ideas for filling in the chart.

CONCLUSION (5 minutes)

- Preview what they will be doing in the next class and remind the students to bring their work plans and Tactic Toolkit.

- Distribute the exit ticket. Call on a student to read the assignment out loud or do this yourself.

- Instruct students to keep their worksheets in their In-Progress GC folder or submit them to you first for grading.

- Have students complete the exit ticket and submit it to you.

ASSESSMENT AND PORTFOLIO ELEMENTS

Exit Ticket: Project Teams

Write down one part you're excited about and one part you're nervous about in working on your tactic.

COMMON CORE STANDARDS

- SL.6-8.1
- SL.9-10.6
- WHST.9-10.7
- SL.9-10.1
- SL.9-10.6
- WHST.9-10.7

WORSHEET

Project Teams

DO-NOW

Word of the Day: _____

Definition: _____

_____

_____

_____

Sample Sentence: _____

_____

_____

_____

My Sentence: _____

_____

_____

_____

Favorite Pick: _____

_____

_____

_____

OVERVIEW AND OBJECTIVES

Your team will begin planning the work you will do to implement tactics that contribute to achieving the goal of the project. Your group will also create specific work plans and assign roles to hold yourselves accountable.

By the end of this lesson, you will be able to:

- work in teams to analyze your tactics;

- create work plans and assign roles.

ACTIVITY

Project Team Work Plan

Instructions: Fill out the table below with the information about your group and your plan for how the group will share responsibility for different parts of the work you need to do to convince your target. Refer to your Target and Tactics Table for the information on key message and tactics for the person assigned to your group.

Names of our team members:

Our target person:

Key message(s) and Ask:

Tactic(s):

What do we need to do?	Who will do it?	By when?
What else will we need to research or learn?		
What are our "measures of success"? (How will we know if we have succeeded?)		

EXIT TICKET

Project Teams

Instructions: Write your response below. Hand this in to your teacher at the end of class.

Write down one part you're excited about and one part you're nervous about in working on your tactic.

_____

_____

_____

_____

_____

_____

LESSON 9+: TAKING ACTION CLASS TEMPLATE

OVERVIEW

After Lesson 9, students will be working in project teams on the specific tactics needed to influence their targeted individual. They will spend part of the day working independently and part of the day in guided teaching time with you. This lesson plan provides a structure for making those sessions as meaningful and productive as possible.

OBJECTIVES

Objectives will likely vary by group, so we recommend drafting group-specific objectives.

MATERIALS

Tactic Toolkit

PREPARATION BEFORE CLASS

- Review each team's progress and prepare any ongoing directions or materials needed.
- If you have distributed only selected sections of the Tactic Toolkit, print and distribute any additional sections students might need.
- Pick a Word of the Day (based on words the groups will likely encounter in their work) and write it and a sample sentence on the board.

> ### Note
> During Unit 3, at a time of your choice, ask students to complete the Group Collaboration Self-Assessment (outside of GC class). They should return the assignment before the following lesson.

LESSON

Introduction (8 minutes)

- *Do-Now:*
  - Have students assemble in their teams and prepare for their check-in.
  - Complete the Word of the Day exercise.
- *Check-Ins:* Remind students that the individual tactics and tasks their groups are working on all contribute to the class's success. As each group checks in, carefully listen to what they have accomplished in case there is the potential to share information or work with other groups.
  - Call on one student to summarize the overall project goal.
  - Ask a representative from each group to share:
    - What they accomplished last period and/or what challenges they faced.
    - What materials they are using.
    - What obstacles they faced/are facing.
    - What they are going to do today.

> *Sample probing questions*
>
> - What are you doing today that might be relevant to another group?
> - Is anything in our goals, Asks, messages, or tactics not working? Do we need to change any of these to improve our chance of success?
> - If you have completed parts of your plan, what else can you do to help the class reach its goal?

Project Teamwork (35 minutes)

- For the first project team meeting and again as necessary:
  - Have students reiterate expectations for small group work.

- Review who is responsible for each task so that students can start the class period with focus (especially for middle school students).

- Remind students that they will be working independently part of the time but that you will spend time with each group to ensure that they are on track. Nevertheless, they should be using their work plan and Tactic Toolkit to do much of the work without your guidance. Point out that the discussion of each tactic includes basic information on the tactic as well as a practice activity that they must complete before applying the tactic to their own situation.

- As students begin working, walk around the room to ensure that all students are at the appropriate Tactic Toolkit pages and on task before focusing attention on one group.

Note

Each tactic in the Tactic Toolkit has several parts: an overview of the tactic, useful information and tips on how to use it, a sample, an exercise to put the abstract into practice, and suggested next steps that students can use to help them bring their efforts to fruition. In the class time in Unit 3, you might direct your students to use these different portions by annotating, taking notes, doing practice questions, creating drafts, and working on next steps.

CONCLUSION (5 minutes)

- Call on each group to find out:
  - What students are doing between this class period and the next.
  - What questions are raised/remain from today's work.

- (When desired) Distribute and review the Group Collaboration Self-Assessment. Remind them that this assessment will become part of their Portfolios.

- Remind students to carefully preserve both their draft and final work on their tactics in their In-Action GC folders so they can decide later which elements to include in their Portfolios.

ASSESSMENT AND PORTFOLIO ELEMENTS

Portfolio:

- As students use particular tactics, ask them to complete the Practice and Drafts associated with them in the Toolkit and keep them in their "In Action GC" folder so that they have these ready to submit if they choose to include that tactic's experience and outcome in their Portfolio.

- Group Collaboration Self-Assessment. Have students complete this independently and return.

Rubrics:

- Generation Citizen Tactic Rubrics: Use the three rubrics to assess the submitted tactics before students place them in their Portfolios. You could distribute the rubrics to students to describe successful work.

- Civic Skills Rubric—Group Collaboration. Use this for grading/assessing before students place the Group Collaboration Self-Assessment in their Portfolios.

Generation Citizen Tactic Rubrics

Below are three general rubrics you can use to assess the tactics assignments. These rubrics focus on the civic skills demonstrated through the different tactics. You can use the written persuasive communication and the critical analysis rubrics for the majority of the tactics. These 2 may be used together. When a student gives a speech or other oral work, you can use the oral persuasive communication rubric along with the critical analysis rubric.

Generation Citizen Civic Skills Rubric—Persuasive Communication (Written)

Criteria		Outstanding/Exemplary	Proficient	Emerging/Developing	Limited/Minimal
Makes a clear and convincing argument	Main idea	Clearly states and empha-sizes an argument or thesis/main idea that is especially unique or com-pelling and uses it to focus writing.	Clearly states argument or thesis/main idea.	Can identify argument or main idea, but it is not clearly stated.	Does not make a clear argument or have a thesis/main idea.
	Organization	Organizes main ideas in a consistently logical yet creative pattern. Con-nects them using effective transitions.	Organizes main ideas in a logical progression (para-graphs, topic sentences, etc.), with a clear introduc-tion and conclusion.	Attempts to organize main ideas logically and may have an introduction or conclusion, but writing is unfocused at times.	Does not have clear orga-nization. Writing is unfo-cused or jumps around, making it difficult to follow.
	Evidence	Persuasively supports ideas with a variety of carefully selected, correctly cited data and reasons. Research on issue and consideration of moral and emotional concerns are evident.	Selects relevant and accu-rate data and reasons to support ideas. Cites sources correctly.	Uses data and reasons to support ideas, but some supporting points may not be relevant or accurate. Evi-dence of research on issue is limited.	Does not support import-ant ideas with data or rea-sons. Research on issue is not evident.
	Other perspectives	Fully addresses other per-spectives, both anticipating and critiquing counterar-guments and explaining how they have influenced thinking.	Addresses other perspec-tives briefly, critiquing other arguments or giving credit to others who have influenced thinking.	Mentions, but does not address, other perspectives on the issue.	Does not consider other perspectives on the issue.
	Audience and purpose	Adapts writing (length, examples, words, style, etc.) to specific needs of pur-pose and audience. Style is particularly creative and effective. Writing inspires audience.	Delivers message through means and length appro-priate for the situation. Lan-guage and examples are generally appropriate.	Some elements of writing (length, examples, words, style, etc.) may be inappro-priate for the audience and purpose.	Gives no consideration to the purpose or audience with regard to the length and means of communi-cation. Uses inappropri-ate language, context, and examples.
Presents argument effectively	Conventions	Spelling and grammar are perfect. Word choice and sentence construction are consistently thoughtful, effective, and inspiring.	Few spelling and grammar errors. Word choice and sentence construction are adequate but not inspiring.	Spelling and grammar errors are common, but writing is understand-able. Appears to pay little attention to the choice of words or construction of sentences.	Writing is difficult to under-stand; issues with spell-ing, word choice, and/or grammar.
	Presentation	Writing package is pol-ished. Elements of presen-tation indicate that writer paid special attention to appearance of piece. Includes other materials (photos, appendixes, etc.) that help to communicate writer's message.	Writing package is attrac-tive and readable.	Writing package is gener-ally readable, but may have unattractive elements.	Writing package is hard to read because of font size or style, handwriting, dam-age, corrections, or other problems.

Generation Citizen Civic Skills Rubric—Critical Analysis

Criteria		Outstanding/ Exemplary	Proficient	Emerging/Developing	Limited/Minimal
Finds, evaluates, and uses information	Identifying sources	Identifies highly relevant sources that express a range of perspectives and are in a variety of formats (books, websites, interviews, etc.).	Identifies relevant sources. Sources may be mostly one format (books, websites, interviews, etc.) and have a limited range of perspectives.	Identifies a few relevant sources. Needs support in determining which are relevant.	Identifies no relevant sources in any format.
	Selecting information	Gathers sufficient, but not extraneous, information from sources. Identifies missing information to find in other sources.	Gathers important information from sources, but may not have enough to make decisions or too much irrelevant information.	Narrows down sources, but needs support to find appropriate information in a source.	Does not narrow down sources or use them to find appropriate information.
	Considering perspective	Considers multiple aspects of a source's perspective, explaining how they influence the information obtained and identifying other perspectives that are needed but not present.	Identifies some aspects of a source's perspective (purpose, point of view, biases). With guidance, can explain how they influence information obtained.	Identifies a source's purpose, point of view, or potential biases with support.	Does not consider source's purpose or point of view.
	Synthesizing sources	Is able to compare and contrast sources and explain reasons for similarities and differences. Makes connections between sources and expresses a synthesized understanding of the issue that is more complex than that expressed by any one source.	Is able to compare and contrast some sources, and explain reasons for similarities and differences on a surface level.	Compares and contrasts some sources with support. Does not give reasons for similarities and differences.	Does not compare, contrast, or synthesize sources.
	Using information	Reflects on and refines own ideas and can explain how information learned affects decisions or actions. Explains how information influences ideas. Use of information is evident in actions and decisions. Continues to seek new information to improve outcomes.	Reflects on or refines ideas with support and uses information to help make decisions or take action.	Uses some information learned to justify decisions or plans for action, but does not reflect on or refine ideas.	Does not reflect on or refine own ideas. Information does not affect decisions.

Generation Citizen Civic Skills Rubric—Persuasive Communication (Oral)

Criteria		Outstanding/Exemplary	Proficient	Emerging/Developing	Minimal/Limited
Makes a clear and convincing argument	Main idea	Clearly states and emphasizes argument or main idea that is especially unique or compelling. Repeats it in a variety of ways.	Clearly states argument or main idea.	Can identify argument or main idea when listening to speech, but it is not clearly stated.	Does not make a clear argument or have a main idea.
	Organization	Organizes main ideas in a consistently logical yet creative pattern. Connects them using effective transitions.	Organizes main ideas in a logical progression, with a clear introduction and conclusion.	Attempts to organize main ideas logically and may have an introduction or conclusion, but speech is unfocused at times.	Does not have clear organization. Speech is unfocused or jumps around, making it difficult to follow.
	Evidence	Persuasively supports ideas with a variety of carefully selected data and reasons from a variety of reputable sources. Research on issue and consideration of moral and emotional concerns are evident.	Selects relevant and accurate data and reasons to support ideas.	Uses data and reasons to support ideas, but some supporting points may not be relevant or accurate. Evidence of research on issue is limited.	Does not support important ideas with data or reasons. Research on issue is not evident.
	Other perspectives	Fully addresses other perspectives, both critiquing arguments and explaining how they have influenced thinking. May thoughtfully consider questions and answer them in a way that enhances argument.	Addresses other perspectives briefly, critiquing other arguments or giving credit to others who have influenced thinking.	Mentions, but does not address, other perspectives on the issue.	Does not consider other perspectives on the issue.
	Audience and purpose	Creatively adapts speech (length, examples, words, style, etc.) to specific needs of purpose and audience. Pays attention to reaction of audience and adjusts speech effectively.	Delivers message through means and length appropriate for the situation. Language and examples are generally appropriate.	Some elements of speech (length, examples, words, style, etc.) may be inappropriate for the audience and purpose.	Gives no consideration to the purpose or audience with regard to the length and means of the communication. Uses inappropriate language, context, and examples.
Presents effectively	Speech	Speaks clearly, naturally, and at an appropriate volume and speed. Expression, conviction, and emphasis create an emotional response in audience.	Speaks clearly, though may occasionally use fillers, sound unnatural, or speak too quickly, slowly, loudly, or softly.	Is generally understandable, but tone, fillers, speed, and/or volume often detract from presentation.	Is hard to hear or understand. Speaks much too quickly, slowly, softly, or loudly.
	Body language	Posture and eye contact are confident, and body language and attire add to the presentation.	Posture and eye contact are generally confident, and body language and attire are appropriate.	Often appears nervous or makes only occasional eye contact. Some aspects of body language or attire are inappropriate.	Does not make eye contact or displays excessive nervous movements. Body language or attire is inappropriate for audience and purpose.
	Materials	Creatively integrates visuals, multimedia, or other relevant, exceptionally high-quality materials with speech to significantly enhance presentation.	Uses relevant, high-quality materials that are easy to see, hear, and understand and add to the speech.	Creates materials that are relevant to the speech, but may be difficult to see, hear, or understand and do not enhance its quality.	Does not prepare visuals, multimedia, or other materials, or materials detract from the content and purpose of the speech.

Group Collaboration Self-Assessment

Instructions: Think about how you are involved in group collaboration as you work on your project. Then answer the following questions:

1. Discuss your biggest strengths or skills when working with a group.

2. Discuss what is difficult about working with a group. Please highlight general group work challenges as well as the ways that you personally struggle when working with a group.

3. Please explain at least one way you can improve your group collaboration skills.

Civic Skills Rubric—Group Collaboration

This rubric can be used to assess the Group Collaboration Self-Assessment any time during Unit 3.

Criteria		Outstanding/ Exemplary	Proficient	Emerging/ Developing	Limited/Minimal
Plays important roles in group	Duties	Completes responsibilities for assigned roles and, at times, facilitates discussion, takes on a leadership role, or helps group reach goals.	Completes responsibilities for assigned roles and takes on a variety of roles within group.	Completes responsibilities for assigned roles, with extra support or prompting at times.	Refuses to take on group roles or does not complete responsibilities for assigned role.
	Attitude	Maintains a positive attitude and encourages others.	Generally maintains a positive attitude.	At times, attitude may negatively influence other group members.	Has a negative attitude toward other group members or the project.
Contributes ideas and listens to others	Ideas	Contributes relevant ideas to discussion, and uses discussion strategies (summary, synthesis, etc.) to keep conversation focused.	Contributes relevant ideas to discussion.	Contributes relevant ideas to discussion if asked.	Rarely contributes relevant ideas to discussion.
	Listening	Listens respectfully and actively to others and asks clarifying questions, synthesizing multiple ideas, and ensuring that everyone has a chance to participate.	Consistently listens respectfully to others. May occasionally ask clarifying questions or build upon someone else's idea.	Listens passively to others. Rarely, if ever, interrupts and can usually explain others' ideas if asked.	Does not show evidence of listening to others' ideas and may interrupt or be disrespectful of others' ideas.
	Feedback	Actively provides and seeks out constructive feedback and incorporates it into work.	Provides and accepts constructive feedback when directed.	Occasionally provides or accepts constructive feedback if directed.	Does not provide or accept constructive feedback.

Helps group reach goals	**Goal setting**	Leads group in setting and/or clarifying goals, compromising if necessary.	Participates in setting and/or clarifying group goals. Eventually compromises if necessary.	Participates in setting and/or clarifying group goals, but may not express opinion or may have difficulty compromising.	Does not participate in setting or clarifying group goals.
	Focus	Consistently stays focused on the group's work and goals. Helps others do the same.	Generally stays focused on the group's work and goals.	Occasionally loses focus on the group's work and goals.	Often loses focus on the group's work and goals.
	Organization	Chooses and adapts effective strategies to organize work.	When directed, uses strategies to organize work (time lines, notes, resource lists, etc.).	When directed, uses strategies to organize work with extra support.	Does not use strategies to organize work.
	Reflection	Encourages group to assess and reflect upon quality of work and progress toward goals.	When directed, reflects on quality of work and progress toward goals.	Reflects on quality of work and progress toward goals with extra support.	Does not reflect on the quality of the group's work.

UNIT 4: TAKING THE NEXT STEP

MAIN GOALS

At the end of Unit 4, students will be able to:

- explain their Advocacy Hourglass and project;
- describe the experience they have had throughout the course and reflect on its effects;
- identify strengths and challenges of working as a team on the action plan;
- analyze both their plan and action to evaluate the successes and/or challenges of each;
- identify ways to continue the work beyond the Generation Citizen class.

Students will have:

- explained and analyzed their action plan and advocacy project;
- analyzed the effect their advocacy project has had on them throughout the course;
- evaluated the strengths and challenges of working as a group;
- identified ways to continue their work beyond the GC class.

UNIT SUMMARY

The final lesson of the curriculum gives students an opportunity to critically reflect on their work and discuss avenues for continued active civic engagement.

REFLECTION AND NEXT STEPS

OVERVIEW

Students will reflect on their semester, discuss the impact of their work beyond the classroom, and connect their experience with ways to continue being civically engaged.

OBJECTIVES

By the end of this lesson, students will be able to:
- describe the advocacy experience and the effect it has had on them throughout the course;
- analyze both their plan and action to evaluate the successes and/or challenges of each;
- identify ways to continue the work beyond the classroom.

WORD OF THE DAY

Reflection (noun): Giving serious thought to something

Sample Sentence: After lengthy reflection on the previous season's successes and failures, the coach decided to change how he ran each practice.

MATERIALS

- . Worksheet: Reflection and Next Steps
- Final Assessment
- Final Reflection

PREPARATION BEFORE CLASS

- Consider what the class will do with the project after the term.
- Print a worksheet, exit ticket, and assessment materials for each student.
- Write the Word of the Day and sample sentence on the board.

LESSON

Introduction (5 minutes)

- *Do-Now:*

    Word of the Day: Reflection

- *Lesson overview and framing*: Explain to the class that today is a chance both to celebrate and to look back on the work they have done and reflect on both the successes and challenges they have experienced—because the point of Generation Citizen is not just to address issues this semester but to develop tools and strategies that will help them address community issues wherever and whenever they find them. Also, the class will talk about how they can continue this project or others in the future.

Looking Back (25 minutes)

- Explain that you also are very interested in hearing about the students' experiences this semester—what they learned and what suggestions they would make for the course in the future.
- Lead students in a discussion of the following questions:
    - What did you learn?
    - How did you change over the course of the semester?
    - What do you know now that you wish you'd known earlier in the course?
    - What did you like about the course?
    - What could be improved?
- If there is time, students can begin to work on the Generation Citizen Final Reflection.

Looking Forward (15 minutes)

- Lead students in a discussion of the following questions:
    - What are some actions you think you could take next with the skills and knowledge you've developed in class?
    - Do you believe that young people can effect change in your community? In what way? Use examples to explain. Do you believe that you can effect change?

- What would you tell students about to embark on a semester of Generation Citizen that you wished you had known before you began?
- Explain that students should keep their worksheets to be able to refer back to all the ideas and descriptions included on them. The worksheets are meant to be a tool not just for this class but for the students anytime they want to begin to work for change on any issue. Explain that what they learned about the Advocacy Hourglass isn't just something they do in a Generation Citizen course—it's a way to use our democracy to initiate change on any issue in our communities.

CONCLUSION (5 minutes)

- Distribute and review the Final Assessment and Final Reflection. Remind students that this assessment will become part of their Portfolios.
- Set expectations and time line for how and when students will complete the compilation of their Portfolio elements and table of contents.
- Thank your students!

ASSESSMENT AND PORTFOLIO ELEMENTS

Portfolio:

- Final Assessment (Instruction Manual): Have students complete the assessment independently outside of class and return it after this lesson.
- Final Reflection (Middle School) or Final Reflection (High School): After this lesson, have students complete this Portfolio element independently outside of class.
- At the end of the course, give students the opportunity (in class or for homework) to go through their In Progress GC folder and put together the elements of the Portfolio they will submit at the conclusion of the program. This should include the following:
  - Table of Contents
  - Introductory Letter (already completed at the start of the course)
  - Unit 1 Assessment (already completed after Unit 1)
  - Unit 2 Assessment (already completed after Unit 2)
  - Group Collaboration Self-Assessment (already completed during Unit 3)
  - Sample Tactic (should include any drafts and a final product)
  - Final Assessment
  - Final Reflection (Middle School) or Final Reflection (High School)

Rubrics:

- Final Assessment Rubric. Use this for grading/assessing the Final Assessment before placing the Assessment in students' Portfolios.
- Final Reflection Rubric. Use this for grading/assessing the reflection before placing the reflection in students' Portfolios.
- Overall Portfolio Rubric. Use this for grading/assessing the full final Portfolio for quality and completion.

COMMON CORE STANDARDS

- SL.6-8.6
- SL.6-8.1
- SL.9-10.6

Name: _____

Reflection and Next Steps

DO-NOW

Word of the Day: _____

Definition: _____

_____

_____

_____

Sample Sentence: _____

_____

_____

_____

My Sentence: _____

_____

_____

_____

Favorite Pick: _____

_____

_____

_____

OVERVIEW AND OBJECTIVES

You will reflect on your semester, analyze the effect of your project, and connect your experience with ways to continue being civically engaged.

By the end of this lesson, you will be able to:

- describe the action process and the effect it has had on you throughout the course;

- analyze both your plan and actions to evaluate the successes and/or challenges of each;

- identify ways to continue the work beyond the classroom.

Final Assessment

An Instruction Manual for Taking Action and Making Change

An instruction manual gives information about how to do something (e.g., use a tool, accomplish a task, assemble parts). Using what you have learned in the course, create a set of instructions for taking action and effecting change that would help the next group of students learn how to follow in your footsteps

Required Elements

Your instruction manual should explain how the next group of students can analyze an issue that matters to them, develop a plan, and determine what actions to take. Include the following elements:

- Use numbers to show the sequence or order of the steps.

- Use and explain any important vocabulary words.

- Mark or describe which parts of the process are good times to look at evidence and why.

- Include stories or details from your own project to give other students examples for different steps.

- Write a creative title for your instruction manual that will get those who read it excited about what they will be learning.

You can create your instruction manual as a numbered list, in paragraphs, or drawn as a flowchart with circles and arrows that will guide the next students through the process.

Final Assessment (Instruction Manual) Rubric

Use this rubric to help you review your own work and as a checklist to make sure that you are including all required elements.

Exemplary/Exceeds Criteria	Proficient/Meets Criteria	Does Not Meet Criteria
Like a "real" instruction manual, process is insightful and creatively combines steps that "work" together. No critical ingredients are missing.	Instructions listed are appropriate to the topic of taking action and include core content and/or concepts. Steps are accurate (e.g., related to civics and action planning).	Basic instructions reflecting understanding of the topic are either missing or have factual errors associated with them.
The mentions of evidence illustrate an understanding of the important role of research and critical analysis at key points in creating and executing the plan.	Mentions of evidence demonstrate an understanding of the general importance of evidence in creating the plan.	Mentions of evidence are not made at appropriate points in the process or fail to convey any sense of importance.
Note: Students can only get a maximum score of "proficient" in this area.	Procedure accurately and logically reflects chronological or sequential steps to follow.	Errors in chronology or lack of coherence in identified sequence of procedure.
Choice of vocabulary and examples, like in a real manual, demonstrates a sense of deeper understanding of how to communicate the experience of taking action.	Procedure vocabulary and examples reflect a basic understanding of how the process of taking action plays out.	Lack of variety in vocabulary and examples indicates lack of understanding of how the process functions to achieve successful action.
Presented in a way that the reader can immediately see the "flow" of the instructions and likely final product.	Procedure has logical coherence in the relationship of various steps.	Procedure lacks coherence.

Manual's title combines accurate portrayal of entire process with cleverness or other forms of insight.	Manual's title summarizes the entire process.	Missing title or title lacks relationship to overall process.
Note: Students can only get a maximum score of "proficient" in this area	Mechanically accurate (e.g., spelling, etc.)	Errors, needs editing, lack of evidence of proofreading.

Comments/Grade:

Final Reflection (Middle School)

Instructions: As the course comes to a close, we ask you to reflect on the action that you and your classmates took and what you learned throughout the process. For this assignment, you can use your worksheets as well as the items you have compiled for your Portfolio to help you answer the following questions in 2–4 full sentences each. To be successful, use specific examples to support your answers.

1. What was most important in what you learned through Generation Citizen?

2. Which lessons or tactics most helped you learn about how to take action? Why?

3. What are you most proud of that you accomplished with Generation Citizen? Was this an individual achievement or one you worked on as a group?

4. Did you actually accomplish the goal of your action plan? In what ways did you or did you not? What did you learn from the experience of success or failure?

5. If you were to continue working on your issue, how would you change or add to your plan?

6. Describe the experience of being part of a group effort. Discuss both the good experiences and the challenges.

7. Do you believe that you and/or young people can cause change to happen in your community? In what way? Use examples to explain.

8. What would you tell students about to start a semester of Generation Citizen that you wish you had known before you began?

Final Reflection (High School)

Instructions: As the course comes to a close, we ask you to write a reflection about the action that you and your classmates took and what you learned throughout the process. For this assignment, you will look over your worksheets as well as the items you have compiled for your Portfolio to help write a reflection using the questions below as a guide.

Please write a one-to-two page reflection that answers at least one question from each of the following categories (and at least five questions total). In your response, note which questions you used.

To be most successful in this reflection, you should use specific examples from your Portfolio work and worksheets.

The Generation Citizen Course

1. What were the most important facts and ideas you learned through Generation Citizen? What did you learn about civic action in Generation Citizen? Why is this important?

2. What are you most proud accomplishing in the course? Was this an individual achievement or one you worked on as a group?

Your Action Plan

3. Did your class create a feasible action plan? How do you know?

4. Did you accomplish the goal of your action plan? In what way? If you did, how did achieving your goal make you feel?

5. If you did not accomplish your goal, why not? What did you learn by not accomplishing your goal that you wouldn't have learned had you accomplished it?

6. What recommendation would you make to the next person or group of people who chose to work on the same issue?

    *   In the future, what are you going to do about the issue your class worked on?

7. Describe the experience of being part of a collaborative (group) effort. Discuss both the good experiences and the challenges.

    *   Did you have to compromise during the process? What was that like for you?

- What happens when parts of a process fail?

8. Describe a time in which there was disagreement in your class about your action plan. Looking back, how was your plan better because you had that disagreement? What did you learn from this?

9. What did you struggle with in your work in Generation Citizen? Discuss something that did not go as well as you had hoped.

   - What did you learn because you had to struggle that you may not have otherwise learned?

   - What would you do differently if you were to do it again?

Your Community

10. In what ways do you see yourself as an important and influential member of your community (local, state, national, or global)?

11. In the future, what would you like to focus on improving? How will you do this?

12. In a democracy, what responsibilities do people have to their community, if any? Use examples to explain.

13. Do you think that young people can effect change in your community? In what way? Use examples to explain. Do you think that you can effect change?

14. What would you tell students about to start a semester of Generation Citizen that you wish you had known before you began?

Final Reflection Rubric

You can use this rubric to assess both the middle school and high school reflections.

	Outstanding/Exemplary 10 points	Proficient 8 points	Emerging/Developing 7 points	Minimal/Limited 0 points
General	Reflection is well-written; includes details and examples.	Reflection includes some details and examples.	Reflection includes only a few examples and very few details.	Reflection does not include details and examples. Reflection is not well written.
	Reflection is linked to and supported by evidence in the Portfolio.	Reflection is sometimes linked to and supported by evidence in the Portfolio.	Reflection is rarely linked to and supported by evidence in the Portfolio.	Reflection is not supported by evidence included in the Portfolio.
	Reflection analyzes own work and identifies and discusses areas of growth and/or learning.	Reflection analyzes own work, but does not discuss areas of growth and/or learning.	Reflection refers to own work, but does not analyze it. Reflection minimally, if at all, discusses areas of growth and/or learning.	Reflection does not analyze own work and does not discuss areas of growth and/or learning.
	Reflection ties the entire Portfolio together in an effective and informative way.	Reflection ties the entire Portfolio together.	It is apparent that the reflection is associated with the Portfolio.	Reflection does not tie the Portfolio together.
	If the student had an opportunity to edit: Reflection has no spelling and/or grammatical errors. Paper is neat and organized.	**If the student had an opportunity to edit:** Reflection has minimal spelling and/or grammatical errors. Paper is neat and organized.	**If the student had an opportunity to edit:** Errors of spelling or grammar and/or sloppy work make paper difficult to read.	**If the student had an opportunity to edit:** Errors of spelling or grammar and/or sloppy work prevent communication of ideas.

Generation Citizen Goals	Reflection demonstrates an understanding of core knowledge and the ability to apply knowledge to different circumstances and settings.	Reflection demonstrates some understanding of core knowledge and some idea of how to apply knowledge to different circumstances and settings.	Reflection demonstrates a minimal understanding of core knowledge and not the ability to apply knowledge to different circumstances and settings.	Reflection does not show an understanding of core knowledge or the ability to apply knowledge to different circumstances and settings.
	Reflection demonstrates that the student knows how to identify, assess, interpret, describe, analyze, and explain matters of concern in civic life.	Reflection demonstrates some ability to identify, assess, interpret, describe, analyze, and explain matters of concern in civic life.	Reflection demonstrates minimal ability to identify, assess, interpret, describe, analyze, and explain matters of concern in civic life.	Reflection does not demonstrate that the student knows how to identify, assess, interpret, describe, analyze, and explain matters of concern in civic life.
	Reflection demonstrates that the student knows how to cope in groups and organizational settings, interface with elected officials and community representatives, communicate perspectives and arguments, and plan strategically for civic change.	Reflection demonstrates that the student knows somewhat how to cope in groups and organizational settings, interface with elected officials and community representatives, communicate perspectives and arguments, and plan strategically for civic change.	Reflection demonstrates that the student has minimal grasp of how to cope in groups and organizational settings, interface with elected officials and community representatives, communicate perspectives and arguments, and plan strategically for civic change.	Reflection does not demonstrate that the student knows how to cope in groups and organizational settings, interface with elected officials and community representatives, communicate perspectives and arguments, and plan strategically for civic change.
	Reflection demonstrates that the student knows the importance of interpersonal and intrapersonal values, virtues, and behaviors as related to citizenship in a democracy.	Reflection demonstrates that the student has some knowledge of the importance of interpersonal and intrapersonal values, virtues, and behaviors as related to citizenship in a democracy.	Reflection demonstrates that the student has a minimal grasp of interpersonal and intrapersonal values, virtues, and behaviors as related to citizenship in a democracy, but may not see them as important.	Reflection does not demonstrate that the student knows the importance of interpersonal and intrapersonal values, virtues, and behaviors as related to citizenship in a democracy.

Total Points: _____/90 (total of 10 possible points for "outstanding" x 9 categories)

Grade:

Overall Portfolio Rubric

Student name:

Total Points:

	Outstanding/ Exemplary 10 points	Proficient 8 points	Emerging/ Developing 7 points	Minimal/Limited 0 points
Organization and Overall Appearance	Portfolio includes all required pieces.	Portfolio is missing 2 pieces.	Portfolio is missing 4 pieces.	Portfolio is missing more than 4 pieces.
	Portfolio assignments are labeled and logically organized.	Portfolio assignments are in a logical order but not labeled.	Portfolio assignments are labeled but not in a logical order.	Portfolio assignments are in no logical order and are not labeled.
	Portfolio reflects time and care invested in preparation, is easily readable, and pleasing to the eye.	Portfolio is easily readable.	Portfolio is readable.	Portfolio is thrown together with little care.
Content	Portfolio content reflects attention to detail: edited and free of errors.	Portfolio has minimal errors.	Portfolio is not edited and has errors that make it difficult to read.	Portfolio is not edited and has many errors that make it very difficult to read.
	Content selected is representative of student's best knowledge and skills.	Some content selected shows some knowledge and skills.	Content is selected with little intent.	Content is randomly selected.
	Content intentionally reflects student growth.	Content shows a little bit of improvement and growth.	Content is consistent, but does not demonstrate growth.	Content does not show growth.

Total Points: _____/60 (total of 10 possible points for "outstanding" x 6 categories)

Grade:

APPENDIXES

APPENDIX A: WORD OF THE DAY PROCEDURES

We recommend the following procedure for Word of the Day:

1. As students enter the classroom, ensure that the Word of the Day (with part of speech) and definition are written on the board or are on the projector, along with instructions to complete the Word of the Day section of their worksheets.

2. In later lessons, where you choose the Word of the Day, be sure that the definition is student-friendly and not copied verbatim from a dictionary. Additionally, if a word has multiple definitions, focus only on the one students will encounter in that day's lesson. For example, a student-friendly definition of "beneficial" might be "helpful/ making good things happen."

3. Write the sample sentence in such a way that someone who did not know the word could easily infer the meaning from the context. The sentence should also use the same form of the word (e.g., adjectival, adverbial) as written in the definition. For example, for "beneficial": Winning the lottery was beneficial for John's family; now they didn't need to worry about how to pay for John's college education.

4. After giving students 2–3 minutes to write down the word, definition, sample sentence, and their own sentence, ask a few students to share their sentences with the class. Again, sentences must use the word correctly, and someone who doesn't know the word should be able to infer its meaning from the sentence. Thus, a sentence like, "Vegetables are beneficial," would not pass muster. If a sentence does not meet those criteria, ask students how the sentence could be improved. (in this case: Vegetables are beneficial to your health because they provide vitamins.)

5. Write several of the students' sentences on the board and have students pick their favorite one to write down in the Word of the Day section of that day's worksheet.

6. *Optional*: You can give occasional vocabulary quizzes. To do so, put the Words of the Day on the board without definitions. Students can then write sentences that use the words in context (again, so that someone could infer their meaning). Conducting and grading such quizzes are quick, easy, and provides an additional opportunity to assess learning (and encourage vocabulary acquisition).

7. Use the Word of the Day when speaking in that day's class and in future ones. Consider pausing and calling on a student to remind the class what the word means. Encountering the word repeatedly and in multiple contexts increases the likelihood that it will become part of students' own lexicon.

8. *Optional*: Put the Words of the Day on a classroom "word wall," so students regularly see and remember them.

APPENDIX B: TACTIC TOOLKIT

This Tactic Toolkit consists of a series of tactics broken down in skill-building segments that allow you to learn and practice skills before drafting and finalizing or using the tactics as part of your action plan. You will likely not complete every tactic in the Toolkit, but will use the sections relevant to your group's tasks. Nevertheless, you should save the Toolkit for reference in case you are involved in advocacy in the future.

Lobbying

Lobbying occurs any time an individual tries to persuade another person of something. In relation to your project, you will need to persuade a decision-maker to take an action that will help you accomplish your goal. You may also need to convince an influencer to support you.

The process of lobbying can take many forms: a written proposal, a formal presentation, a letter, or even a conversation with a decision-maker. To lobby effectively, you must create and deliver a persuasive argument.

Useful Information

Designing an Argument with Your Decision-Maker in Mind

Effective arguments are based on what will persuade your audience.

- Always identify a specific person to target and then tailor your argument to him or her. Ask yourself: What are her priorities? What is her history on this or related issues? Who or what is she responsible for? Who or what influences her opinion?

- Strengthen your argument using different methods of persuasion: ethos, logos, and pathos.

  - **Ethos** is an appeal based on the character or experiences of the speaker (e.g., Michael Jordan is a spokesman for a basketball shoe. You want to buy the shoe because if he says it is a good shoe, you assume he is right.).

  - **Logos** is an appeal based on reason. A logos-driven argument relies on facts and logic (e.g., convincing a friend that smoking is dangerous because 24% of heavy smokers develop lung cancer).

  - **Pathos** is an appeal based on emotion; a pathos-driven argument taps into shared feelings or values (e.g., defending a school from closure because it's a central part of the neighborhood and community members feel a strong personal connection to it.)

Practice

Instructions: Identify whether each argument relies primarily on ethos, logos, or pathos.

_____ A commercial solicits money for a hospital by flashing pictures of children with cancer on screen.

How do you know? _____

_____ A magazine ad shows Kim Kardashian selling expensive perfume.

How do you know? _____

_____ A billboard for the Department of Health explains how far you would have to walk to work off the calories from one Big Mac.

How do you know? _____

Practice

Instructions: Analyze the sample testimony of Sam Adams, a Boston public school student, who spoke to the Boston City Council and answer the questions below.

Good afternoon, honorable Council members, and thank you for hearing my argument today on behalf of my class as representatives of Boston Public School District students. I attend Boston Arts Academy as an upcoming sophomore dance major. I'm here to talk about recycling throughout BPS and the critical impact of improving the district's recycling program.

Recycling is not being prioritized throughout Boston Public Schools and this creates a negative cycle of an uncaring culture, lack of knowledge about the impacts of waste, and no effort to make a positive change. I am here today to try to convince you of the need to implement single-stream recycling across the district as a major step forward in driving our schools to reduce their footprint and educate students about the value of recycling.

Single-stream recycling programs have been implemented in school systems, government departments, and businesses in many communities in our state and country. Their efficiency for users and reduction of waste should not be underestimated. From the research my class has done in our school and by talking to administrators, we know that logistical barriers are some of the biggest reasons that people do not use the limited recycling resources available to us now.

Our education should not just be about math and English. My classmates and I should have role models in our school and district administrators who show us the way to be environmentally responsible citizens who care about the future of our planet. If we do not see adults who care about this issue in our schools where we spend most of our days, we are missing an opportunity to get this kind of education.

Boston could set an example for other cities and become a district that instills values of protecting and sustaining the environment for its children and our future generations. Let's not fall behind.

Thank you.

1. Who are the decision-makers Sam Adams is targeting? Why is he targeting them?

2. What is the issue on which he is speaking?

3. What is his position—what does he ask his audience to do?

4. Find a use of logos in the testimony. Do you find it effective? Why or why not?

5. Find a use of pathos in the testimony. Do you find it effective? Why or why not?

Useful Information

Structuring an Effective Argument

Use the following structure to design a persuasive argument:

- **Issue:** Introduce the topic, hooking the decision-maker with an introduction based on ethos, logos, or pathos.

- **Position:** Take a stand; make your Ask—what you want your decision-maker to do.

- **Points:** Present your key points or messages to convince your decision-maker based on your ethos/logos/pathos approach.

- **Counterpoints:** Address potential objections or disagreements the decision-maker might have.

- **Conclusion:** Restate your position.

Sample Structuring an Argument

Issue	The airlines' use of fuel is one of the fastest-growing sources of pollution linked to climate change on the planet. For 15 years, the airlines have dodged regulation.
Position	Please support reducing pollution from aviation by opposing Senator John Thune's bill S.1956, which bars U.S. airlines from complying with Europe's pollution controls.
Points	A traveler flying from London to New York and back generates about as much carbon pollution as the average person in the European Union (EU) does by heating a home for a whole year. Emissions from flights in and out of Europe have doubled since 1990 and are growing fast.
	An EU requirement to cut pollution from flights between the United States and Europe will drive new technologies and spur demand for more fuel-efficient airplanes that can be built right here in the United States. It will reduce our nation's dependency on oil and imports. By 2020, the EU law will cut carbon pollution by an amount equivalent to taking 30 million cars off the road.
Counterpoints	Some might argue that the movement towards fuel-efficient aviation will end up costing the travelers unreasonable fairs and fees. In fact, the cost to each passenger is negligible—a fraction of what the airlines already charge for checking a bag, for example. With no global agreement to reduce carbon pollution from the aviation sector, bringing these emissions under Europe's existing emission's cap is a sensible first step. But U.S. airlines want none of this. Instead of stepping up to the plate to lead on the global warming challenge, the airlines are asking you to enact the bill S.1956. That's not leadership. And, it's not a way to solve differences between countries about pollution.

Conclusion	Please support cleaner aviation, U.S. jobs, and the environment, by opposing S.1956.

Adapted from "Take Action: Stand up Against Aviation Pollution." https://secure2.edf.org/site/Advocacy?cmd=display&page=UserAction&id=1985. Used by permission.

Template: Persuasive Lobbying Argument

Complete the steps below to research your influencers or decision-maker(s). Then use the template to draft your argument in this format.

1. Research your influencers or decision-maker(s) to determine: What are their priorities? What is their history on the issue? Who or what are they responsible for? Who or what influences them?

2. Decide which methods of persuasion (ethos/logos/pathos) your decision-maker(s) will find most convincing and compile appropriate evidence

Decision-maker(s)	
Issue and approach (ethos, pathos, logos)	
Position	
Points	
Counterpoints	
Conclusion	

Tips for Running a Lobbying Meeting

- Always speak face-to-face, if possible—this is the most effective way to lobby.

- To schedule a meeting, contact the decision-maker with a formal call or email briefly stating who you are, what you would like to discuss, how much time it will take, and suggested times and locations at which you are available. Be prepared to work around the schedule of a decision-maker who may have limited availability.

- One-to-two days before the scheduled meeting, call to confirm the time and place.

- When planning a meeting, make sure it has a clear goal, structured agenda, and a plan for follow-up:

  - A goal identifies what you want from your decision-maker by the end of the meeting (which may or may not be your entire "Ask").

  - An agenda (outlining introductions and your argument) keeps you on track during the meeting.

  - To follow up, send an email to the decision-maker thanking her for her time, restating your key messages, and reviewing identified next steps.

- Dress professionally.

- Shake hands and make eye contact when introducing yourself.

Next Steps You Could Take with Your Project Team

1. Edit and strengthen your argument.

2. Contact your decision-maker to schedule a meeting.

3. Prepare a meeting goal and agenda and determine who will present which sections of the agenda.

4. Confirm your meeting time and place one-to-two days before it is scheduled.

5. Practice delivering your argument and edit appropriately.

6. Conduct your meeting.

7. Send a follow-up email immediately after the meeting.

8. Create a summary or visualization of the lobbying argument and lobbying process to be shared with others.

9. Put your drafts and final products in your In-Progress GC folder.

10. Collaborate with another relevant project team.

Letters, Calls, and Emails

Hearing from constituents, or the people for whom they are responsible, helps decision-makers take a position on an issue and prioritize which issues they will spend their time and energy on. An effective way for you to make your voice heard is to send letters to, call, or email decision-makers. This is a particularly useful strategy for influencing elected officials.

Useful Information

Running a Letter/Call/Email Campaign

For a letter/call/email campaign to be effective, communication must include *variety* and *volume*:

- Let them hear a *variety* of voices—do not rely on form letters or strict scripts; quality counts, so make the communication personal when possible.

- Let them hear from a *variety* of people—use your coalition or influencers to demonstrate wide support from people of different ages, backgrounds, or interests.

- Let them hear *enough voices* to demonstrate deep support ("enough" depends on your decision-maker).

Writing a Letter/ Email/ Call Script

Your goal is to convince your decision-maker that this issue matters to you and affects the community. An effective script will include:

- **Issue:** Explain the topic to be discussed.

- **Position:** Take a stand; make your Ask—what you want your decision-maker to do.

- **Points:** Present your key points based on evidence.

- **Conclusion:** Restate your position and thank the decision-maker for his or her time.

Sample Letter/Email Script

	Mrs. Rainone's Current Events Class Hope High School, Class of 2010 324 Hope St. Providence, RI 02906 Dear Representative Ajello,
Issue	We, the students of Mrs. Rainone's Current Events class from Hope High School, are submitting this letter to underscore the issue of hunger in the state of Rhode Island.
Position	As constituents in your district, we ask for your support in continuing to effect change to combat this problem by sponsoring a bill to add the Rhode Island Community Food Bank as a charitable contribution option on the RI personal income tax form.
Points	We are approaching this problem from multiple angles. Our class has coordinated a food drive with the Rhode Island Community Food Bank, to which all food collected will be donated. We have written letters and contacted different organizations to secure additional donations for the Rhode Island Community Food Bank. In an effort to evaluate current awareness of the issue, we have also conducted a survey to test the extent to which Hope students are affected by hunger and their awareness of the scope of the problem. However, with all this work, we recognize that our efforts could be much more successful if we could make supporting the RI Community Food Bank easier for more people. A spokesperson from the Food Bank, Michael Cerio, said "with this struggling economy, the need is 50 percent greater than it was three years ago. The Food Bank is helping more than 55,000 people in Rhode Island every month." If we can pass an amendment to the state law titled "Reciprocity Agreements—Setoff of Personal Income Tax," we could allow Rhode Islanders to donate a portion of their state income tax refund to the Rhode Island Community Food Bank. This could increase the amount, number, and sustainability of much-needed donations and reduce hunger for residents of our state.

Conclusion	We are asking that you support our proposal, which involves Rhode Island's current personal income tax form. We have noticed that RI-1040 has a contributions section; we are hoping to have another line added to this section that would allow taxpayers to contribute to the food banks of Rhode Island. This would allow taxpayers to donate one, five, ten, or more dollars to these food banks. This would be an important addition to the tax form because of its convenience to taxpayers and would result in food banks receiving more contributions, which is especially crucial in this period of economic recession.
	Thank you for your time and consideration,
	Mrs. Rainone's Current Events Class

Sample Call Script

Issue	Hello, I am a student calling from Hope High School, a school in Representative Ajello's district. I am calling to speak with Representative Ajello about the issue of hunger in the state of Rhode Island.
Position	I ask that you sponsor a bill to amend the state law titled "Reciprocity Agreements—Setoff of Personal Income Tax" so that, on the RI personal income tax return (form RI-1040), we could add another line to the charitable contribution options that would allow taxpayers to contribute to the food banks of Rhode Island. This would allow taxpayers to donate one, five, ten, or more dollars to these food banks.
Points	In the current struggling economy, according to Michael Cerio from the Rhode Island Community Food Bank, "the need is 50 percent greater than it was three years ago. The Food Bank is helping more than 55,000 people in Rhode Island every month."
	This would be an important addition to the tax form because of its convenience to taxpayers and would result in food banks receiving more contributions, which is especially crucial in this period of economic recession.

Conclusion	I ask that you agree to support and/or sponsor a bill to amend this law to give residents a ready and sustainable way to help reduce hunger in our state. This would have a major impact on the resources available to food banks that feed so many of our state's residents.

Tips for Writing Letters and Email

For Writing a Letter

- At the top of your letter, include a full heading so that you can be contacted:
    Date
    Your Street Address
    Your City/State/Zip Code
    Your Email Address
    Your Phone Number

- Be brief and clear—a short letter is more likely to be read than a long one.

- Personalize—the more genuine or "real" it is, the more seriously it will be taken.

For Writing an Email

- Use a strong subject line: reference the issue or legislation and point you are making (e.g., "Support" is less meaningful than "Support for Anti-Bullying Bill").

- Personalize—if it reads like a SPAM message, it is not likely to be taken seriously.

- After "Sincerely," include the following information:
    Your Name
    Your Street Address
    Your City/State/Zip Code
    Your Phone Number

For Your Call

- If you cannot reach your decision-maker, explain who you are, ask when a good time to call would be, and if there is someone else you could speak with. Try calling back at different times and send an email with your messages.

- Be polite, yet let your decision-maker know you're serious about the issue.

- Have potential responses prepared in case your decision-maker asks questions or wants to learn more about your ideas.

- Send the person with whom you spoke a follow-up thank you email.

Practice

Instructions: Analyze the sample email and answer the questions that follow.

Dear Senator James:

As a constituent and a student at Roosevelt High School in Greyville, Illinois, I wanted to write to ask you to support more restrictions on gun purchases in our state and the enforcement of existing laws.

Since I started high school two years ago, I have seen the tragic shooting of two classmates who were my age and were victims of gun violence in our neighborhood. This is not the kind of experience that we should have when we are trying to safely attend school, gain an education and try to find jobs, and participate in our community.

Although the Brady Handgun Violence Prevention Act requires background checks for firearms purchased from federally licensed gun dealers and our state has various regulations about the types of background checks and licensing required for gun ownership, I know that not all individuals who want to own a gun go through the legal channels.

I want to make sure that people in my community and in the communities across our state are held accountable for getting all proper background checks before purchasing guns. I hope you will see the pressing need for increased security around these sales and support us in pushing for legislation that will increase regulations specifically for private gun sales so that we can limit illegal access to these deadly weapons.

Sincerely,

Maria Gonzales

---

1. How does Maria demonstrate that she cares about the issue?

2. What is Maria asking Senator James to do?

3. Summarize one point that Maria makes supporting her position.

4. How can the senator get back in touch with Maria? What is missing, and where should it go?

Template: Letter/Call/Email Script

Complete the steps below to research your influencers or decision-maker(s). Then use the template to help you draft your script.

1. Identify your decision-maker.

2. Decide whether you want to send an email or letter or make a call (or any combination).

3. Draft your communication.

(Greeting)	
Issue	
Position	
Points	
Conclusion	

Next Steps You Could Take with Your Project Team

1. Edit your scripts into a final format.

2. Collect appropriate contact information (addresses, phone numbers, email addresses)

3. Send letters and emails and make calls.

4. Solicit more letters/emails/calls from influencers.

5. Create a summary or visualization of the scripts or products to be shared with others.

6. Put your drafts and final products in your In-Progress GC folder.

7. Collaborate with another relevant project team.

Writing a Survey

Surveys are a way to collect data about an issue and to gauge people's opinions so you can address your issue most effectively.

Useful Information

Writing a Survey

An effective survey is *relevant* and *accurate*.

- It has a clear purpose and has questions that align with the purpose.

- It is brief, easy to understand, and unbiased.

- It is relevant to the people responding.

Tips for Writing a Survey

- Think backwards: when you are writing survey questions, identify who will take the survey and who will read the results. Then think about how to word your questions. For example, if I want to convince my school principal that we need healthier cafeteria food, I want to ask students questions to determine if they are satisfied with the cafeteria's healthy food options rather than ask them what their favorite snacks are.

- Keep questions short and ask them one at a time; don't try to fit two questions into one.

- Avoid "loaded" or "guiding" questions that imply what the desired answer is (e.g., "Don't you think that our school SAT prep really stinks?)—don't use emotional or overtly positive/negative language to direct your respondents to a certain answer.

- Be precise. To get the most accurate information, avoid words like "generally" or "often." Instead be more direct with phrases like "once per week" or "every day."

- Keep your survey short; answering the questions should be easy and painless.

- Vary the question types—make some open-ended and others multiple choice.

- Don't use overly difficult vocabulary or unprofessional slang.

Practice

Instructions: Analyze the survey and answer the questions below.

1. What do you define as "bullying"?

2. Have you ever been bullied? (circle one)

    Yes   No   Decline to answer

3. Have you ever witnessed bullying? (circle one)

    Frequently   Often   Rarely   Never

4. Have you ever bullied someone else? (circle one)

    Frequently   Often   Rarely   Never

5. How much do you talk to or text with other students in class?

6. How often do you witness bullying at school? (circle one)

    More than 1 time a day   1 time a day   1–2 times per week   3–4 times per week   never

7. Teachers don't do anything to help with bullying. Why do you agree or disagree with this statement? (circle all that apply)

    They are too busy.

    They don't care.

    They don't know that bullying is occurring.

    They are scared of the bullies.

8. If the school had harsher consequences for bullies, then the amount of bullying in school would decrease. (circle one)

    Strongly agree   Agree   I don't know   Disagree   Strongly disagree

9. Bullying is a problem at our school. (circle one)

Strongly agree   Agree   I don't know   Disagree   Strongly disagree

10. Why is bullying a problem at our school? What can we do to help it?

11. If I were a teacher I would stop jerks from bullying. (circle one)

Yes   No   Decline to answer

---

1. What might be the purpose or objective of this survey?

2. Are there any questions that do not align with that objective? Which ones?

3. Are there any questions that are unclear? Which ones?

4. Are there any questions that are biased or direct you to choose one answer? Which ones?

5. Which questions do you find to be the most effective, and why?

6. Is there any difficult vocabulary or slang?

7. Does the survey use a variety of different questions?

8. On scale of 1 (very ineffective) to 10 (very effective), how would you rate this survey, and why?

Template: Draft a Survey

Answer the questions below before drafting your survey questions.

1. What is your survey's purpose or objective? _____

2. Who will be completing the survey? _____

3. What kinds of information will you need to achieve your objective? _____

Use the following checklist to review your survey.

Survey Checklist

☐ My survey has a clear objective (I know how I am going to use my information).

☐ I know what information I need.

☐ All of my questions are aligned with my purpose/point.

☐ My survey is relevant. The people I am surveying will have answers to my questions.

☐ My questions are clear and concise.

☐ I ask one question at a time.

☐ My questions are easy to answer and unbiased.

☐ I have an appropriate number of questions.

☐ My language is clear. I have defined all vocabulary and avoided slang.

☐ My survey contains a variety of question types (open-ended, multiple-choice, etc.).

Adapted from Survey Monkey's "Smart Survey Design" http://s3.amazonaws.com/SurveyMonkey Files/SmartSurvey.pdf. Used by permission.

Next Steps You Could Take with Your Project Team

1. Edit your survey by going through the survey checklist and making any necessary changes.

2. Determine what time and place is best to administer your survey and the number and type of people you will survey.

3. Coordinate logistics to administer surveys (make copies, get any necessary approvals, etc.).

4. Administer your survey.

5. Carefully collect your data.

6. Analyze your data.

7. Prepare your data to be shared with appropriate project teams and appropriate decision-makers.

8. Create a summary or visualization of the survey and survey process to be shared with others.

9. Put your drafts and final products in your In-Progress GC folder.

10. Collaborate with appropriate project teams.

Holding a Public Meeting

Public meetings are used to educate, influence, and/or mobilize large numbers of people (decision-makers, influencers, and the public), or even to generate media attention. A public meeting might take the form of a town meeting, school assembly, panel discussion, or workshop, to name a few settings.

Useful information

Staging a Public Meeting

A public meeting needs to be planned effectively and should have the following components:

- clear goal (aligned with your overall project goal)

- structured agenda

- task list for those preparing the meeting with clear division of responsibilities and deadlines for completion

- strategic meeting time to ensure all participants can attend (for example, trying to get parents to meet during the workday would not be successful)

- carefully selected meeting venue with sufficient space for all participants and permission from the venue managers/administrators

- prepared materials

- advertising

Tips for Holding a Public Meeting

- To advertise effectively, identify and focus your attention on where your target audiences typically find out about community news and events (newspapers, blogs or online community announcements, bulletin boards, newsletters, flyers).

- When developing posters and advertisements, remember to include the title, date, time, and location of the event.

- Plan advertisements in advance so that they can be placed in a timely manner.

Practice

Instructions: Analyze the following event preparation sheet and answer the questions below.

Organization: Ms. May's 11th-grade American History class

Project Goal: Increase teen jobs around the campus community

Event: School-wide jobs fair

Event Goal: Educate students about job opportunities in the area and put them in contact with local employers

Event Details: Friday, 10/19/2014, 3–5 pm, Central High School Auditorium

Task	Person(s) Responsible	Completion Date
Set up approval meeting with AP Myers	Carlos	October 5
Organize and prepare presentation for AP	Alex, Danielle, Trey	October 5
Make presentation to AP	Carlos, Alex, Danielle, Trey	October 8
Contact Chamber of Commerce	Carlos	October 9
Call employers	Carlos, Alex	October 10
Make event agenda	Danielle, Trey	October 10
Design and print fliers	Trey	October 12
Draft and send out press release	Danielle	October 12
Put announcement in school paper	Alex	October 15
Put up fliers	Whole class	October 15
Send employers confirmation emails	Carlos, Alex	October 16
Create and print programs	Danielle, Trey	October 17
Distribute event agenda to teachers	Carlos, Alex, Danielle, Trey	October 18
Set up tables, chairs, microphones	Whole class	October 19

---

1. How does this event benefit the overall project?

2. Why did they arrange a meeting with Assistant Principal Myers?

3. What materials do they need for their event? Where might they get them?

4. Who did they have to contact to plan the event?

5. Which tasks needed to be completed first? Why?

6. Which tasks could wait until closer to the event? Why?

7. Where should they advertise?

8. What information should they include in their advertisements?

9. What kind of follow-up might they want to do after the event?

10. Why was assigning individuals to be responsible for different tasks important?

Template: Public Meeting Preparation Task List

Use the template to help you draft your preparation task list.

Organization:		
Project Goal:		
Event:		
Event Goal:		
Event Details:		

Task	Person(s) Responsible	Completion Date

Next Steps You Could Take with Your Project Team

1. Edit your Event Prep Sheet.

2. Secure event venue and finalize logistics.

3. Finalize who will lead each portion of event.

4. Create advertising and other materials and post advertising.

5. Walk through the event itself.

6. Create a summary or visualization of the event to be shared with others.

7. Put your drafts and final products in your In-Progress GC folder.

8. Collaborate with another relevant project team.

Holding a Coalition Meeting

A coalition meeting can be a critical part of your action plan. Building coalitions (a group of people who agree to cooperate for a joint cause or action) demonstrates to decision-makers that key individuals or groups support your issue. To build a successful coalition, you have to convince people to join the cause. The best way to do this is to have a face-to-face meeting.

Useful Information

Identifying Coalition Partners

To identify potential coalition partners, think about:

- Who might support your cause?

- Who is able to influence your decision-maker?

The people or groups in both categories are good potential partners for your coalition.

Enlisting Coalition Partners

When tailoring your argument to potential partners, consider the following:

- What is their relationship to the decision-maker?

- What are their priorities?

- What is their history on this or related issues?

- Who or what are they responsible for?

- How will their involvement in the coalition benefit them?

- Why might they hold back or hesitate to join?

Use the following structure to design an effective argument for a potential partner:

- **Issue:** Introduce the topic to be discussed, describing common ground between your interest and their organization.

- **Position:** Make your "Ask"—what you want your coalition partner to do.

- **Points:** Present your key points to convince your coalition partner based on your understanding of his or her priorities, history, and responsibilities.

- **Counterpoints:** Address your coalition partner's potential hesitations.

- **Conclusion:** Restate your position and points.

Sample Coalition Partner Identification Table

Focus Issue	Lack of jobs available to teens in our neighborhood
Root Cause	Citywide curfew prevents students from holding a range of available jobs
Goal	Convince the City Council to extend the curfew from 10 pm to 11 pm on weeknights
Decision-maker(s)	The city council member from our district
Potential Coalition Partners	Business owners, parents (PTA), employment-focused nonprofits

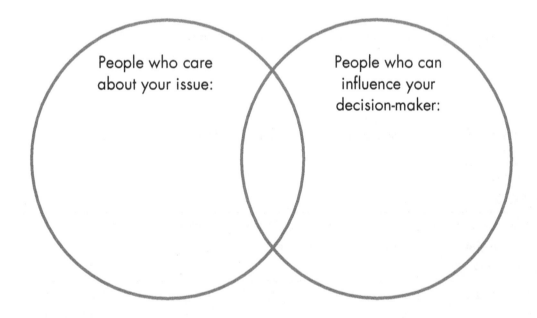

Tips for Planning a Coalition Meeting

- Always speak face-to-face, if possible.

- To schedule a meeting, contact the potential partner with a formal call or email briefly stating:

  - who you are

- what you would like to discuss

- how much time it will take

- suggested times and locations at which you are available and an invitation for the partner to suggest alternatives

- One-to-two days before the scheduled meeting, call to confirm the time and place.

- When planning a meeting, make sure it has a clear goal, structured agenda, and a plan for follow-up.

  - A goal identifies what you want from your coalition partner by the end of the meeting.

  - An agenda keeps you on track during the meeting.

- Dress professionally.

- Shake hands and make eye contact when introducing yourself.

- To follow up, send an email to the meeting's participants thanking them for their time, restating your main argument, and reiterating identified next steps.

Practice

Instructions: Read the following example and answer the questions below.

POTENTIAL PARTNER	Business owner
What is the relationship to the decision-maker?	Businesses owners drive the local economy, which the council members are interested in and are responsible for promoting.
What are their priorities?	Business owners care about having an affordable and available labor force, low taxes, safe neighborhoods to encourage customers, steady customer base…
What is their history on this or related issues?	(From research) In 2008, business owners lobbied the city council to lower fines for working with undocumented workers; they care about inexpensive labor.
What are they responsible for?	Selling their products or services

How will their involvement in the coalition benefit them?	Supporting our cause will potentially give them access a broader pool of available labor.
Why might they hold back or hesitate to join?	They might be nervous about other young people staying out late and loitering outside of their stores, thus scaring other potential customers away.

Coalition Partner Meeting Agenda

(Welcome)	Thank you so much for meeting with us. We know you are busy and appreciate your fitting us into your schedule.
Issue	Our 9th-grade history class, through a program called Generation Citizen, is working to create and identify more jobs for teens in our community. We think that one way to accomplish this would be to extend the citywide curfew on weeknights. This would benefit students by giving them access to more work opportunities and employers like yourself by expanding your labor pool.
Position	We would like your help in passing a city ordinance extending the curfew from 10 to 11 pm. We would like for you to help us put pressure on the city council to pass this ordinance. We are scheduled to speak before the city council at their next meeting, November 14, at 7:00 pm. If you could join us there and say a few words, we know it would strengthen our case before the council.
Points	After conducting a school-wide survey, we found that 70% of our peers work or have worked part-time. In addition, 60% say that they would like to work more if given the option. The current curfew precludes students from a range of jobs, as after-school shifts often require helping to close stores and restaurants late at night—after the current curfew.

If students can stay out later, they will be able to work more shifts. Businesses would benefit from having more applicants for their positions, and with a larger number of applicants, employers can be sure |

	they will find strong candidates for their openings. Also, as young people stay out later, they will certainly visit local shops and restaurants, providing additional income for local businesses. Extending the curfew serves to benefit both Baytown students and businesses.
Counterpoints	Some opponents warn that a later curfew will promote delinquency among Baytown's youth. However, if the curfew were extended, our research leads us to believe that more teens would be employed and therefore be off the streets.
Conclusion	We believe this ordinance will help to create employment that will benefit both Baytown students and businesses. We know your support will go a long way with the city council. We hope you will join us on November 14, and we thank you for your time.

1. How do the students forge a common bond with their audience (business owners)?

2. What is the class's position? What are they asking the business owners to do?

3. What is the business owners' potential hesitation which the students address?

4. Why do you think it is important that the students thanked the business owners at the beginning and end of the meeting?

5. What should the students do next to follow up?

Template: Identify Potential Coalition Partners

Use this template to outline the information you will use to identify potential coalition partners.

Focus Issue	
Root Cause	
Goal	
Decision-maker	
Potential Coalition Partners	

People who care about your issue:

People who can influence your decision-maker:

Template: Analyze Coalition Partner

Use this template to help you analyze your potential coalition partners and to tailor your arguments for each.

Potential Coalition Partner(s)	
What is their relationship to the decision-maker?	
What are their priorities?	
What is their history on this or related issues?	
Who or what are they responsible for?	
How will their involvement in the coalition benefit them?	
Why might they hold back or hesitate to join?	

Template: Agenda for a Coalition Meeting

Use this template to help you draft the agenda for your meeting.

Welcome	
Issue	
Position ("Ask")	
Points	
Counterpoints	
Conclusion	

Next Steps You Could Take with Your Project Team

1. Call or email potential partners to request a meeting.

2. Compose and edit your draft agenda.

3. Determine who will participate in the meeting and present each part of the argument.

4. Practice and give feedback on delivering the arguments.

5. Present the arguments to your potential coalition partners.

6. Follow up from meeting with a call, letter, or email.

7. Create a summary or visualization of the meeting to be shared with others.

8. Put your draft agenda and final products from your meeting in your In-Progress GC folder.

9. Collaborate with another relevant project team.

Using Social Media

Social Media includes web-based and mobile technologies such as Facebook, Twitter, You-Tube, blogs, or anything that turns communication into an interactive experience between users. You can use social media to generate publicity for an event, raise awareness on an issue, and interact with supporters and keep them informed about your group and your issue.

Useful Information

Using Social Media

- Set a goal for your social media campaign.

- Identify platforms that your targeted audiences already use.

- Update content regularly with a variety of posts, multimedia, and authors, including news from your campaign and relevant articles/information.

Tips for Using Social Media

- Stay on message.

- Ask questions to get conversations started.

- Provide links to related resources and information.

- Use multimedia (videos, photos) to keep readers engaged.

- Connect people with one another through links.

- Publicize any updates via your other social media platforms.

- If you are setting up a blog, pick the most useful platform (e.g., WordPress, Blogger, Jux, Tumblr, etc.).

Practice

Instructions: Analyze the examples and answer the questions below.

Example 1: Social Media Posts

Organization: Healthy Children Org

Organization Goal: To help children in the United States and around the world live enriched and healthy lives

Facebook excerpt

 Helping Children Org shared a link

> Every 2 minutes a woman dies of complications in pregnancy.
> If you feel passionately about the future of every girl and woman, please sign and spread this pledge:
>
> **http://sampletest/DKndk**

Twitter Excerpt

 Helping Children Org @HelpingKidsNow
We're helping #children & families affected by the Monsoon in the #Phillipines: http://linktothepagesample

 Building a Better World Org @wecanmakeitbetter
Taping video #2 for @helpingkidsnow- this is by far the most exciting collaboration we've had http://linktotheimagesample

 Helping Children Org @HelpingKidsNow
We need your support to give "ordinary" kids a chance to be awesome at #debate: http://linktothepagesample

 Jennifer Mills @jennjennmi
Going to a meeting today with the team at @helpingkidsnow http://linktothepagesample

---

1. Who might be included in the target audience of this social media campaign?

2. What are the main messages conveyed in the organization's social media postings?

3. Does Healthy Children's campaign do a good job of engaging people through multimedia, references, and links? How?

4. Do Healthy Children's social media do a good job of connecting people and keeping readers engaged? How?

Example 2: Blog Posts

Organization: Generation Citizen

Organization Goal: To engage young people in solving problems in their own communities by learning about and using political action

July 30, 2013

HOW IT ALL HAPPENS

This coming school year, Generation Citizen will grow to serve more students than ever across our sites. Growth is both exciting and a challenge – and that requires a better understanding of precisely how GC empowers students – and how we can do better.

GC recently commissioned a research study by two experienced independent evaluators, Rebecca Silvo and Jonathan Thomas. The study utilized extensive student and teacher interviews to better understand how our program leads to student outcomes (civic knowledge, skills, motivation/dispositions).

Here is just one of many student quotes on the power of GC to empower students and put them on a path to future civic engagement:

"All of us can really relate to problems that happen outside [the school], but we didn't know that everyone was having these problems. When we found out it was happening to a whole bunch of people, we thought it was a really big issue and we wanted to fix it. We started doing more research which made us more interested."

You can download the study here to learn more. Please consider reading it today, and letting us know your thoughts.

- Alison Collins, Research and Evaluation Consultant to Generation Citizen

---

August 15, 2013

NADIA'S LAW PART 3: IT LAUNCHED!

Nadia's Story: Recycling in Boston Public Schools

I've been thrilled to share with my Greater Boston classes a recent example of youth making change: the passage of single-stream recycling in Boston Public Schools, a move very much accelerated by a Generation Citizen student from Boston Arts Academy, Nadia Ossan.

The story?

- **Part 1: We Should Call it Nadia's Law:** Last spring, GC student Nadia Ossan makes an appeal for recycling in schools at Generation Citizen's Civics Day. Inspired, Civics Day guest Councilor Felix Arroyo files a hearing order to launch single stream recycling across the entire district.

- **"Nadia's Law": Part 2:** The hearing takes place, and the Committee on Education supports a plan by BPS Facilities and the Center for Green Schools to launch a single-stream recycling initiative across 50 BPS schools for the 2012-2013 school year, with the aim of expanding to all 125 BPS schools by next fall.

- **The Launch:** BPS goes forward with the proposed initiative this past September 2012. Mayor Thomas M. Menino rings in the event with a special ceremony at Blackstone Elementary. See below for a video of Mayor Menino kicking off single-stream recycling:
http://www.cityofboston.gov/cable/video_library.asp?id=2831

The Moral of the Story?

Yes, change can be hard, change can be slow, and can be daunting as a young person. But don't let yourself think that change is impossible.

- Gillian Powers, Greater Boston Program Manager at Generation Citizen

1. Was the blog updated regularly? When was it updated? How do you know?

2. What types of posts were included? (news, stories, events, etc.)

3. Were all posts by the same author or different authors? What types of people contributed?

4. How does the blog take advantage of multimedia and social media (pictures, videos, links, comments)?

5. Do you think Generation Citizen's blog is effective? Why or why not?

Template: Social Media Campaign

Use this template to help you draft your social media campaign plan. Remember that you can decide which social media outlets you will use and adjust the number of columns you need accordingly.

Goal(s)				
Target Audience(s)				

	Facebook	Twitter	Blog	Other
Purpose				
Potential Contributors				
Possible Information/ Topics				
Deadline(s)				
Person(s) Responsible				

Next Steps You Could Take with Your Project Team

1. Edit your social media plan.

2. Compile content for different media in each column you will use.

3. Enlist others to participate.

4. If technology is available, create appropriate platforms (Facebook page, Facebook event, Twitter account, blog).

5. Solicit feedback from classmates about the effectiveness of various platforms.

6. Create a visualization of social media you can share with others.

7. Put your drafted plan and final products in your In-Progress GC folder.

8. Collaborate with another relevant project team.

Writing an Op-Ed

"Op-ed" stands for "opposite the editorial page." Newspaper editors share their opinions on the editorial page. On the facing page, editors allow the public and regular columnists to submit their thoughts. Newspapers often publish op-eds by authors who are experts in their field.

NOTE: Letters to the editor and op-eds are both opportunities for regular people to be published: letters to the editor are short responses to specific articles; op-eds present longer opinions on larger issues.

Useful Information

Writing an Op-Ed

An effective op-ed includes a:

- *Title*: captures the audience's attention in a few words;

- *Lead*: draws the reader into caring about the issue with a "hook," a means of attracting interest. Hooks can vary widely but some of the most common are:

  - A human interest story

  - Shocking or powerful numbers/statistics

  - A focus on local and/or timely issues (how the problem affects your and the readers' community)

  - Controversy

  - A situation to which most readers can immediately relate;

- *Problem*: explains the issue and why it is a problem; include statistics and other relevant evidence and research;

- *Solution*: describes what you think should be done about the issue;

- *Counterpoint*: anticipates potential arguments that opponents might raise and explains and provides reasoning for your disagreement;

- *Conclusion/Call to Action*: reiterates how and why the reader should get involved.

Tips for Writing an Op-Ed

- Requirements vary, so check your specific news outlet, but most op-eds are between 500 and 800 words.

- Time the submission of your op-ed to coincide or directly follow relevant news or events that touch on your message—you'll have a better chance of getting published.

- Submit your op-ed to several news outlets but recognize that it should only be published in one; thank the outlet if your piece is published.

Sample Op-Ed

Lead	A few months ago, after months of debate and negotiations, health insurance reform passed in Congress—the biggest social reform in decades. Yet youth—who will be affected as much as anyone by the new bill—were barely aware that a national debate was even occurring.
Problem	The frenetic 24-hour news cycle has young people hearing more about Sarah Palin's latest Facebook posting than about substantive issues like health care, unemployment, the war in Afghanistan, and potential school budget cuts.
	This has wide-ranging repercussions. Scholars have found that students who are more civically engaged tend to have higher levels of motivation and self-efficacy and also perform better academically. When students address social problems, they recognize that their schoolwork is not only important to pass standardized tests, but that such engagement allows them to be leaders in their communities and take action on issues they care about.
Solution	If we are serious about combating the growing political inequality in this country, effective civics education for every student in this country is a must.
	First, schools must recognize that civics is an interdisciplinary subject and that it cannot be studied in a vacuum. To become effective citizens, students must be able to read, write, and communicate effectively. It is completely possible, and necessary, to plan effective, engaging civics classes while aligning curricula to standards and preparing students for standardized tests.

	Second, civics education must be engaging. Students learn math by repeated practice in solving math problems; they learn science by conducting experiments. Students should not study civics just by learning about the three branches of government, they should also engage in the political process by actually acting on issues of concern.
Counterpoint(s)	Effective and engaging civics education will not solve all of our political and educational problems. The reasons for this gap are complex, with no simple solution. Effective, engaging civics education during the school day, however, is a strategy with promise.
Conclusion/ Call to Action	As school starts this fall, we must make a renewed effort to engage all of our youth in the political process. The next generation has the promise and potential to solve many of the problems plaguing American society; our duty is to help empower them with the skills they need to be active, effective citizens.

—Peter Levine, CIRCLE, Tufts University, MA |

Adapted from: http://www.huffingtonpost.com/peter-levine/educating-youth-for-bette_b_743345.html. Used by permission.

Practice

Instructions: Read the following op-ed and label its:

1. lead

2. problem

3. solution

4. counterpoint

5. conclusion/call to action

Then answer the questions below.

> The students of EBC High School for Public Service in the Bushwick community are appalled about the state of our school lunches.

Insufficient food and poor-quality food are discouraging and distracting students throughout the school day; it seems that the issues with school lunches are citywide and affect the 1.1 million students in the Department of Education school lunch program. If more money were provided for the school lunch program, the quality of food and of education would improve. Students are noticing that expiration dates are being ignored on dairy products. Fruits are not being replaced and lose their freshness, discouraging students from picking up a healthy snack instead of a candy bar or bag of chips. School lunches lack the necessary flavor, variety, and quantity that promote healthier eating by children and teens.

The food served in New York City public schools is also negatively affecting students' stamina in class and their long-term educational progress. Meals lack protein, vitamins, and calories, which are essential for a healthy diet. Each student is different—for example, students who play sports need more calories to maintain their strength and stamina in games. Even students who don't play sports need energy to maintain focus in classes. Hunger can affect grades, test scores, and even students' health. Instead of concentrating on lessons, they're listening to growling stomachs and wondering about the next possible meal.

This funding could come out-of-pocket—as many students have done before when breaking their alliance with the school food program. The problem is that working-class parents, who work hard to make ends meet and often receive help from government organizations, do not have the necessary funds to provide their children with daily lunch. The money could be raised, but how long until it runs out? It doesn't seem right, and we need a long-term solution.

For us to get better and more-filling food, we need to increase funding. As little as a few more cents per meal can make the difference between a reheated slice of pizza and a healthier choice such as a piece of fish or some vegetables. We are confident that it is not just the students at EBC High School who feel this way. This is something that affects us all as students, teachers, parents, and citizens of the United States.

—*Carlos Perez, Herbert Loma, Jonathan Sanchez, Charina Torres, and Heaven Vallejo are students at EBC Bushwick High School for Public Service, NY.*

1. How does the lead catch your attention and convince you to keep reading?

2. Summarize the authors' main points about why school lunches are an important issue.

3. What is the authors' proposed solution?

4. What possible counterpoint(s) do the authors raise?

5. What does the authors do in their conclusion to end on a powerful note?

Template: Op-Ed

Use this template to help you draft your op-ed.

Title: _____

_____

Lead: _____

_____

_____

Problem: _____

_____

_____

Solution: _____

_____

_____

Counterpoint: _____

_____

_____

Conclusion/Call to Action: _____

_____

_____

Next Steps You Could Take with Your Project Team

1. Edit your op-ed into final format.

2. Create a list of local news organizations, including op-ed page editors' contact information.

3. Send out your op-ed to identified news outlets.

4. Follow up on your submission with a phone call to the news outlet to check progress.

5. Share published op-ed via other media (blog, Facebook, Twitter).

6. Create a summary or visualization of the op-ed and writing process to be shared with others.

7. Put your drafts and final products in your In-Progress GC folder.

8. Collaborate with another relevant project team.

Writing a Media Advisory or Press Release

Media advisories and press releases are announcements sent to news outlets to encourage media coverage of an event or issue.

A media advisory briefly addresses the who, what, when, where, and why of an event. It announces and provides details of the event in advance.

A press release is a short news story that you write about your event, usually after the fact. Sometimes, media will publish press releases, or portions of them, as articles.

Useful Information

- When writing a media advisory:

  - You can attract an audience by listing the names and titles of those speaking at your event or community leaders who will be attending.

  - The first paragraph of your media advisory should briefly set out who, what, when, where, and why. You'll expand on each of those points in the following paragraphs.

  - Be sure to structure the body of your media advisory around concise and clear answers to who, what, where, when, and why.

- When writing a press release:

  - The opening sentence is the most important of a press release; it is where you succinctly summarize what you are announcing. The opening paragraph should clearly get the reader's attention through a strong hook while also answering who, what, when, where, and why.

  - The body of your press release should consist of three-to-six paragraphs in which you expand on the information in the introductory paragraph and provide all of the information a reporter needs to write a story, including quotes from important people involved in your project. The average press release is no more than 500 words.

  - List the most important information first, with the least important information appearing in the final paragraph. Each paragraph should consist of 3–6 sentences written in the third person. Remember to maintain an objective tone.

  - Be sure to run the release through spell-check and to fact-check your information.

Tips for Writing a Media Advisory or Press Release

1. Use information on audience and history of coverage to identify media outlets that are likely to cover your issue.

2. Identify specific reporters to contact.

3. Send a media advisory to reporters 3–5 days before your event/desired day of coverage as well as on the morning-of.

4. Call reporters to confirm they have received your advisory and will cover the event.

5. Immediately after the event, send your press release to reporters and call to confirm its receipt.

Sample Media Advisory

FOR IMMEDIATE RELEASE
11/2/2015

For more information, please contact: James Wilson, 222-345-6000, jwilson@email.com

Media Advisory

Students Lead Training on Preserving Providence

Students from Knight High School in Providence, RI, will be kicking off a series of workshops open to the public about the regulations for preserving Providence's historic neighborhoods and resources available for community members to learn more about how to participate in protecting and maintaining historic buildings. Following the kick-off event Saturday Feb 28th at 6 pm at City Hall, the workshops will be held each Saturday in March from 10 am-noon at the Knight High School cafeteria. The workshops are part of the class's work with Generation Citizen to educate their community about the legal protections for their neighborhood and engage them as stewards for the future.

Who: Hosted by Generation Citizen; Special Guest: Mayor Angel Taveras

What: Youth Preserving Providence Kick-Off event and workshop signup

When: February 28th, 2015. Keynote remarks, 6 pm. Refreshments and workshop sign up 6:30 pm.

Where: Providence City Hall, 25 Dorrance St, Providence, RI 02903, 1st floor

---

Why: Event to kick off Youth Preserving Providence workshop series. Sign-up opportunity for workshops to learn more about preservation regulations and resources for involvement.

Speakers: Mayor Angel Taveras; Generation Citizen Executive Director, Scott Warren.

###

FOR IMMEDIATE RELEASE   CONTACT: Sarah Anderson
                                         555-555-5555, sarah@email.org

Broad Based NYC Coalition Urges Mayor to Prioritize Youth Civic Engagement

Youth-serving organizations from across New York City come together to appeal to Mayor Bill de Blasio

NEW YORK, NY, January 15, 2014— In the wake of Mayor Bill de Blasio's election as Mayor of New York, a group of civic and educational organizations from across the city gathered in Manhattan to advocate for measures that will increase youth political participation and civic engagement in New York City. The coalition held its first public meeting this week after issuing a public memorandum to the Mayor where they presented a set of five concrete policy proposals specifically designed to increase youth political participation.

The coalition presented their ideas to Bill de Blasio to persuade him to take action symbolically, on a city level and at a state level. Some of their requests include ensuring that civics education is further incorporated into school curricula, advocating lowering the voting age to 17 in local elections, supporting legislation allowing 16- and 17-year-olds to serve on community boards, and promoting voter pre-registration legislation. The memo's authors include the Sadie Nash Leadership Project, Resilience Advocacy Project, the Roosevelt Institute-Campus Network, and Generation Citizen along with several others.

In their case to the Mayor, the coalition noted that "despite youth interest in the election, we are sure you are aware that this election saw only 24% of eligible voters participate, the lowest turnout in over 50 years. . . . This is especially pronounced amongst young people: millennials, or 18- to 29-year-olds, accounted for only 11% of voters in 2013." They explained that "part of the problem is that we are not prioritizing youth civic engagement and education; we are not educating our young people toward becoming effective participants in our democracy" and urged Mayor de Blasio to take action based on their policy recommendations.

MAKING CIVICS RELEVANT, MAKING CITIZENS EFFECTIVE   •   TACTIC TOOLKIT

The coalition intends to continue diverse advocacy efforts to engage other elected officials, educational institutions, and local philanthropies to spread this priority across the state.

###

Practice

Instructions: Analyze the following media advisory and answer the questions below.

FOR IMMEDIATE RELEASE
May 11, 2013

Media Advisory

Mayor Thomas M. Menino to Host 200 Students at Boston Civics Day

Students Will Present Their Ideas on How to Improve Boston

During Boston Civics Day, 200 middle and high school students will gather at the State House to present their ideas for a better Boston to Mayor Thomas M. Menino. Students will have big ideas to share after learning about civic engagement through their schools' partnership with Generation Citizen.

Elected officials and community leaders will serve as judges, awarding prizes and providing feedback to help the students' ideas become reality. Mayor Menino will address the students and receive Generation Citizen's "Citizen of the Year Award."

WHO: Boston Mayor Thomas M. Menino, Representative Gloria L. Fox, Malden Mayor Gary Christenson, other elected officials, along with more than 200 middle school and high school students from 14 schools.

WHEN: Friday, May 11, 11:30 AM–2:00 PM

About Generation Citizen
Founded in 2008 by Scott Warren, then a Brown University senior, Generation Citizen is a nonprofit organization that empowers young people to effectively address problems in their own communities. Through a comprehensive action civics course, students are guided by trained college-student volunteers who partner with middle and high school teachers and use an innovative peer-to-near-peer mentorship approach. During the semester-long program, students learn what it means to be an effective and engaged citizen and come to

realize that they can be agents of change. Generation Citizen currently works with more than 6,000 young people in low-income schools in Boston, Providence, and New York City. For more information, visit www.generationcitizen.org.

###

1. Identify three important items that this media advisory is missing.

2. The date given at the upper left-hand corner is incorrect. On what dates should this media advisory have been sent to reporters?

3. Do you think that this media advisory is effective in giving information to reporters and in explaining why they should come to the event? Why or why not?

Instructions: Analyze the following press release and answer the questions below.

PRESS RELEASE

FOR IMMEDIATE RELEASE

Contact: Daniel Millenson, Generation Citizen, (555) 555-5555

Hundreds of NYC Students Present their Ideas on Improving New York at Civics Day

"We Get the Opportunity to Help Make Things Right"

Senator Squadron Keynote; Elected Officials, Community Leaders Judge Civics Ideas

NEW YORK, May 4 – Seniors at the High School for Public Service in Crown Heights were fed up with their unhealthy lunch options: whether it was cafeteria grub or the local fast food joint, seniors Brittney Harris and Ahmed Askar were hungry for something different. Along with their classmates, they are launching a food cart initiative that will provide healthier, affordable options to students who will no longer need to leave campus for nutritious eats.

Suma Aftan attends the all-female Urban Assembly School for Criminal Justice in Borough Park – and realized that many young women at her school lacked the vital health information to protect themselves in relationships. So she and her fellow 9th graders have designed and proposed a mandatory women's health course to be incorporated into the school's curriculum. "In this class we get the opportunity to help make things right," Aftan observed.

In Astoria at IS 204 Oliver W. Holmes School, Ibrahim Hadid's 8th grade class had had enough of muggings by drunken neighborhood loiterers, who sipped booze on the streets from brown paper bags. So he and his classmates have approached their local city council member to boost fines on public drinking and toughen enforcement so they can get home safely from school.

These are just a few of the 200 middle and high school students who competed in the second annual spring New York Civics Day, sponsored by the nonprofit Generation Citizen, at the Smithsonian National Museum of the American Indian. Generation Citizen works with middle and high school students from lower-income neighborhoods to help them learn how they can have an impact on their community and government. Over the course of this semester, 700 students from 14 schools in all 5 boroughs have worked to use the democratic process to take action on issues they care about. Or, as Aftan puts it, "Generation Citizen gives us the opportunity to build new ideas about what we change in order to make the world a better place."

Elected officials and community leaders served as judges, awarding prizes and providing feedback to help the students' ideas become reality. State Senator Daniel Squadron (D-Lower Manhattan) keynoted the event and addressed the students.

1. Identify two important points that the author makes to the reader about the event.

2. On what date should this press release be sent to reporters?

3. Explain one thing that you like or dislike about this press release and how that will either help or hurt coverage of this event.

Template: Media Advisory

Use this template to help you draft your media advisory.

FOR IMMEDIATE RELEASE
Date

For more information, please contact: [Contact name, title, phone number, email]

Media Advisory

Headline for Event (*One sentence—be creative. Capitalize every major word.*)

The lead paragraph of your media advisory body should very basically answer the questions of who, what, when, where, and why. You'll expand on each of those points after the opening.

Who: The host group/organization and other participants

What: Brief title or description of your event

When: Day, date of event, time p.m. or a.m., and schedule of event

Where: Site and address of event, room or floor

Why: The purpose of your event

Speakers (optional): List the names and titles of speakers or other community leaders who are supporting this effort and will be present

Background information (optional): Additional background information about the group, organization, or initiative

###

Template: Press Release

Use this template to help you draft your press release.

FOR IMMEDIATE RELEASE   **CONTACT:** [Contact name, title,
                                             phone number, email]

(Headline) _____

(CITY, State, Month Day, Year) _____

(Body) _____

-30-

Next Steps You Could Take with Your Project Team

1. Collaborate with appropriate project teams to verify event/issue details.

2. Edit your media advisory.

3. Create a list of local news organizations, including relevant reporters' contact information.

4. Contact reporters and send out media advisories. Edit and send out press release.

5. Create a summary or visualization of the media advisory, press release, and publicity-gathering process to share with others.

6. Put your drafts and final products in your In-Progress GC folder.

Writing a Letter to the Editor

Letters to the editor give ordinary citizens the opportunity to have personal responses to articles published in newspapers and magazines.

Letters to the editor and op-eds are both opportunities for readers to offer their thoughts on an issue. Letters to the editor are short responses to specific articles; op-eds present lengthier opinions on larger issues.

Useful Information

Writing a Letter to the Editor

- Research local and relevant news outlets for articles related to your issue.

- An effective letter to the editor is concise and timely. Use the following structure to design an effective letter:

  - **Greeting:** The standard greeting is "To the Editor,"

  - **Comment on article:** Make a brief comment on the article setting out your position on the issue

  - **Reasons:** Provide clear reasons to support the letter's position

  - **Conclusion:** End with a summary and/or recommendation and a final catchy line

  - **Signature:** Include first and last name, job title, city, date of response

Tips for Writing a Letter to the Editor

- When referencing an article, put the title in quotation marks and include the date it was published in parenthesis (for example, "Finding Lessons in the Cheating at Stuyvesant" (June 27).

- Newspapers often limit letters to the editor to two-to-three paragraphs and 250–300 words.

- Feel free to question another's opinion in your letter, but avoid personal attacks.

- Include a name, address, and daytime and evening phone numbers with your submission so that you can be contacted if your letter is chosen for publication.

Sample Letter to the Editor

Greeting	To the Editor,
Comment on Article	Friday's article, "Sex Encouraged with Comprehensive Education," (April 14) questioned the effect of comprehensive sex education on sexual activity. Many people worry that giving youth accurate information about sexual health will encourage them to have sex, but this isn't so.
Reasons	Studies have proven that those of us who receive comprehensive sex education are more likely to delay sexual activity and to use contraceptives when we do become sexually active. Even the Surgeon General has declared that it is "imperative and clear that [youth need] accurate information about contraceptives." Yet, the current administration chooses ideology over science and spends millions of dollars on ineffective and inaccurate abstinence-only programs.
Conclusion	The Responsible Education about Life (REAL) Act would provide states with funding to implement school-based sex education that includes information about both abstinence and also contraception. It is imperative that we urge Congress to support the REAL Act.
Signature	Sincerely, Shanice Manning 11th-grade honors student at West Elm High School Baltimore, MD, April 16

Adapted from "Writing a Letter to the Editor," Advocates for Youth, http://www.advocatesforyouth.org/sercadv/245?task=view. Used by permission.

Practice

Instructions: Analyze these letters to the editor and answer the questions below.

Letter A

To the Editor:

This article strikes a harsh chord for me as a graduate of a local university and current employee of a small local business. We need to broaden the discussion to consider the wider disparities between those who do and do not attend college.

College offers opportunities and education far beyond the paper degree and formal major. It gives students from all walks of life the opportunity to learn from one another, collaborate, develop long-term relationships, and examine the beliefs they learned in their hometowns and from their parents. In today's economy and society, are these not ultimately important in developing the next generation of knowledge and creative workers and citizens?

We need to consider the longer-term effects not just of lower lifetime earnings, but of the loss of a rich opportunity to educate the next generation in critical thinking, communicating across differences, and developing nuanced and individual opinions about the world. When we think about this problem, we need to look further than the dollar signs.

Sandra Lowry
Berkeley, Calif., August 6, 2012

Letter B

To the Editor:

Re: "Financial Effects of College Attendance" (page 10, Aug. 5)

Monday's article "Financial Effects of College Attendance" offers a compelling and challenging perspective on the lifetime earning disparities between college graduates and those who have not had the opportunity to continue their education past high school. It seems that our society and educational institutions need to take a hard look in the mirror to recognize their role in this gap and all its consequences.

When will employers, government, and universities recognize their own responsibility in this matter? While non-college-going students need rich and engaging options, the bigger problem is that many students who do want to attend higher education institutions are being halted by the ever-rising tuition and insurmountable surrounding expenses of everything from applications to textbooks.

If the "powers that be" do not take steps to improve this situation and to create meaningful financial aid opportunities to address the spectrum of costs affiliated with college attendance, we are doomed to stifle the potential of our nation's next generation before they even get off the ground. The effects of this will affect all of us if we don't take action.

Todd Belmore,
Bolton, NY, November 6, 2013

1. What is the title of the article to which these letters are responding?

2. When was the original article published?

3. What is Letter A's idea about what should be done?

4. What is Letter B's idea about what should be done?

5. What is missing from Letter A?

6. Do you consider Letter A or Letter B to be more effective? Why?

Template: Letter to the Editor

Use this template to help you draft your letter to the editor.

To the Editor,

Comment on article: _____

_____

Reasons: _____

_____

Conclusion: _____

_____

Sincerely,

Signature: _____

Next Steps You Could Take with Your Project Team

1. Edit your letter.

2. Submit your letter to the appropriate news outlet to be published.

3. Follow up on your submission with a phone call to the news outlet to check progress.

4. Share published letters via other media (blog, Facebook, Twitter).

5. Create a summary or visualization of the letter and letter-writing process to be shared with others.

6. Put your drafts and final products in your In-Progress GC folder.

7. Collaborate with another relevant project team.

APPENDIX C: NATIONAL COMMON CORE STANDARDS

English Language Arts Common Core High School Standards

Speaking and Listening

http://www.corestandards.org/the-standards/ELA-Literacy/

Comprehension and Collaboration

SL.9-10.1

Initiate and participate effectively in a range of collaborative discussions (one-on-one, in groups, and teacher-led) with diverse partners on grades 9–10 topics, texts, and issues, building on others' ideas and expressing their own clearly and persuasively.

- Come to discussions prepared having read and researched material under study; explicitly draw on that preparation by referring to evidence from texts and other research on the topic or issue to stimulate a thoughtful, well-reasoned exchange of ideas.

- Work with peers to set rules for collegial discussions and decision-making (e.g., informal consensus, taking votes on key issues, presentation of alternate views), clear goals and deadlines, and individual roles as needed.

- Propel conversations by posing and responding to questions that relate the current discussion to broader themes or larger ideas; actively incorporate others into the discussion; and clarify, verify, or challenge ideas and conclusions.

- Respond thoughtfully to diverse perspectives, summarize points of agreement and disagreement, and, when warranted, qualify or justify their own views and understanding and make new connections in light of the evidence and reasoning presented.

SL.9-10.2

Integrate multiple sources of information presented in diverse media or formats (e.g., visually, quantitatively, orally) evaluating the credibility and accuracy of each source.

Presentation of Knowledge and Ideas

SL.9-10.4

Present information, findings, and supporting evidence clearly, concisely, and logically such that listeners can follow the line of reasoning and the organization, development, substance, and style are appropriate to purpose, audience, and task.

SL.9-10-.5

Make strategic use of digital media (e.g., textual, graphical, audio, visual, and interactive elements) in presentations to enhance understanding of findings, reasoning, and evidence and to add interest.

SL.9-10.6

Adapt speech to a variety of contexts and tasks, demonstrating command of formal English when indicated or appropriate.

Reading History and Social Studies

http://www.corestandards.org/the-standards/english-language-arts-standards/history-social-studies/grades-9-10/

Key Ideas and Details

RH.9-10.1

Cite specific textual evidence to support analysis of primary and secondary sources, attending to such features as the date and origin of the information.

RH.9-10.2

Determine the central ideas or information of a primary or secondary source; provide an accurate summary of how key events or ideas develop over the course of the text.

RH.9-10.3

Analyze in detail a series of events described in a text; determine whether earlier events caused later ones or simply preceded them.

Craft and Culture

RH.9-10.4

Determine the meaning of words and phrases as they are used in a text, including vocabulary describing political, social, or economic aspects of history/social science.

RH.9-10.5

Analyze how a text uses structure to emphasize key points or advance an explanation or analysis.

RH.9-10.6

Compare the point of view of two or more authors for how they treat the same or similar topics, including which details they include and emphasize in their respective accounts.

Integration of Knowledge and Ideas

RH.9-10.7

Integrate quantitative or technical analysis (e.g., charts, research data) with qualitative analysis in print or digital text.

Writing in History, Social Studies, Science and Technical Subjects

http://www.corestandards.org/the-standards/english-language-arts-standards/writing-hst/grades-9-10/

Text Types and Purposes

WHST.9-10.1

Write arguments focused on discipline-specific content.

- Introduce precise claim(s), distinguish the claim(s) from alternate or opposing claims, and create an organization that establishes clear relationships among the claim(s), counterclaims, reasons, and evidence.
- Develop claim(s) and counterclaims fairly, supplying data and evidence for each while pointing out the strengths and limitations of both claim(s) and counterclaims in a discipline-appropriate form and in a manner that anticipates the audience's knowledge level and concerns.
- Use words, phrases, and clauses to link the major sections of the text, create cohesion, and clarify the relationships between claim(s) and reasons, between reasons and evidence, and between claim(s) and counterclaims.
- Establish and maintain a formal style and objective tone while attending to the norms and conventions of the discipline in which they are writing.
- Provide a concluding statement or section that follows from or supports the argument presented.

WHST.9-10.2

Write informative/explanatory texts, including the narration of historical events, scientific procedures/experiments, or technical processes.

- Use precise language and domain-specific vocabulary to manage the complexity of the topic and convey a style appropriate to the discipline and context as well as to the expertise of likely readers.

Product and Distribution of Writing

WHST.9-10.5

Develop and strengthen writing as needed by planning, revising, editing, rewriting, or trying a new approach, focusing on addressing what is most significant for a specific purpose and audience.

WHST.9-10.6

Use technology, including the Internet, to produce, publish, and update individual or shared writing products, taking advantage of technology's capacity to link to other information and to display information flexibly and dynamically.

Research to Build and Present Knowledge

WHST.9-10.7

Conduct short as well as more sustained research projects to answer a question (including a self-generated question) or solve a problem; narrow or broaden the inquiry when appropriate; synthesize multiple sources on the subject, demonstrating understanding of the subject under investigation.

WHST.9-10.8

Gather relevant information from multiple authoritative print and digital sources, using advanced searches effectively; assess the usefulness of each source in answering the research question; integrate information into the text selectively to maintain the flow of ideas, avoiding plagiarism and following a standard format for citation.

WHST.9-10.9

Draw evidence from informational texts to support analysis, reflection, and research

Range of Writing

WHST.9-10.10

Write routinely over extended time frames (time for reflection and revision) and shorter time frames (a single sitting or a day or two) for a range of discipline-specific tasks, purposes, and audiences

Writing

http://www.corestandards.org/the-standards/english-language-arts-standards/writing-6-12/grade-9-10/

Text Types and Purposes

W.9-10.1

Write arguments to support claims in an analysis of substantive topics or texts, using valid reasoning and relevant and sufficient evidence.

- Introduce precise claim(s), distinguish the claim(s) from alternate or opposing claims, and create an organization that establishes clear relationships among claim(s), counterclaims, reasons, and evidence.

- Develop claim(s) and counterclaims fairly, supplying evidence for each while pointing out the strengths and limitations of both in a manner that anticipates the audience's knowledge level and concerns.
- Use words, phrases, and clauses to link the major sections of the text, create cohesion, and clarify the relationships between claim(s) and reasons, between reasons and evidence, and between claim(s) and counterclaims.
- Establish and maintain a formal style and objective tone while attending to the norms and conventions of the discipline in which they are writing.
- Provide a concluding statement or section that follows from and supports the argument presented.

W.9-10.2

Write informative/explanatory texts to examine and convey complex ideas, concepts, and information clearly and accurately through the effective selection, organization, and analysis of content.

- Introduce a topic; organize complex ideas, concepts, and information to make important connections and distinctions; include formatting (e.g., headings), graphics (e.g., figures, tables), and multimedia when useful to aiding comprehension.
- Develop the topic with well-chosen, relevant, and sufficient facts, extended definitions, concrete details, quotations, or other information and examples appropriate to the audience's knowledge of the topic.
- Use appropriate and varied transitions to link the major sections of the text, create cohesion, and clarify the relationships among complex ideas and concepts.
- Use precise language and domain-specific vocabulary to manage the complexity of the topic.
- Establish and maintain a formal style and objective tone while attending to the norms and conventions of the discipline in which they are writing.
- Provide a concluding statement or section that follows from and supports the information or explanation presented (e.g., articulating implications or the significance of the topic) or section that follows from and supports the information or explanation presented.

English Language Arts Common Core Middle School Standards

Speaking and Listening

http://www.corestandards.org/the-standards/english-language-arts-standards/speaking-and-listening-6-12/grade-8/

SL.8.1

Engage effectively in a range of collaborative discussions (one-on-one, in groups, and teacher-led) with diverse partners on grade 8 topics, texts, and issues, building on others' ideas and expressing their own clearly.

- Come to discussions prepared having read or researched material under study; explicitly draw on that preparation by referring to evidence on the topic, text, or issue to probe and reflect on ideas under discussion.
- Follow rules for collegial discussions and decision-making, track progress toward specific goals and deadlines, and define individual roles as needed.
- Pose questions that connect the ideas of several speakers and respond to others' questions and comments with relevant evidence, observations, and ideas.
- Acknowledge new information expressed by others, and, when warranted, qualify or justify their own views in light of the evidence presented.

SL.8.2

Analyze the purpose of information presented in diverse media and formats (e.g., visually, quantitatively, orally) and evaluate the motives (e.g., social, commercial, political) behind its presentation.

Presentation of Knowledge and Ideas

SL.8.4

Present claims and findings, emphasizing salient points in a focused, coherent manner with relevant evidence, sound valid reasoning, and well-chosen details; use appropriate eye contact, adequate volume, and clear pronunciation.

SL.8.5

Integrate multimedia and visual displays into presentations to clarify information, strengthen claims and evidence, and add interest.

SL.8.6

Adapt speech to a variety of contexts and tasks, demonstrating command of formal English when indicated or appropriate.

Reading History and Social Studies

http://www.corestandards.org/the-standards/english-language-arts-standards/history-social-studies/grades-9-10/

Key Ideas and Detail

RH.6-8.1

Cite specific textual evidence to support analysis of primary and secondary sources.

RH.6-8.2

Determine the central ideas or information of a primary or secondary source; provide an accurate summary of the source distinct from prior knowledge or opinions.

RH.6-8.3

Identify key steps in a text's description of a process related to history/social studies (e.g., how a bill becomes law, how interest rates are raised or lowered).

Craft and Structure

RH.6-8.4

Determine the meaning of words and phrases as they are used in a text, including vocabulary specific to domains related to history/social studies.

RH.6-8.5

Describe how a text presents information (e.g., sequentially, comparatively, causally).

RH.6-8.6

Identify aspects of a text that reveal an author's point of view or purpose (e.g., loaded language, inclusion or avoidance of particular facts).

Integration of Knowledge and Ideas

RH.6-8.7

Integrate visual information (e.g., in charts, graphs, photographs, videos, or maps) with other information in print and digital texts.

Writing in History, Social Studies, Science and Technical Subjects

http://www.corestandards.org/the-standards/english-language-arts-standards/writing-hst/grades-6-8/

Text Types and Purposes

WHST.6-8.1

Write arguments focused on discipline-specific content.
- Introduce claim(s) about a topic or issue, acknowledge and distinguish the claim(s) from alternate or opposing claims, and organize the reasons and evidence logically.
- Support claim(s) with logical reasoning and relevant, accurate data and evidence that demonstrate an understanding of the topic or text, using credible sources.
- Use words, phrases, and clauses to create cohesion and clarify the relationships among claim(s), counterclaims, reasons, and evidence.
- Establish and maintain a formal style.

- Provide a concluding statement or section that follows from and supports the argument presented.

WHST.6-8.2

Write informative/explanatory texts, including the narration of historical events, scientific procedures/ experiments, or technical processes.

- Use precise language and domain-specific vocabulary to inform about or explain the topic.

Production and Distribution of Writing

WHST.6-8.4

Produce clear and coherent writing in which the development, organization, and style are appropriate to task, purpose, and audience.

WHST.6-8.5

With some guidance and support from peers and adults, develop and strengthen writing as needed by planning, revising, editing, rewriting, or trying a new approach, focusing on how well purpose and audience have been addressed.

WHST.6-8.6

Use technology, including the Internet, to produce and publish writing and present the relationships between information and ideas clearly and efficiently.

Research to Build and Present Knowledge

WHST.6-8.7

Conduct short research projects to answer a question (including a self-generated question), drawing on several sources and generating additional related, focused questions that allow for multiple avenues of exploration.

WHST.6-8.8

Gather relevant information from multiple print and digital sources, using search terms effectively; assess the credibility and accuracy of each source; and quote or paraphrase the data and conclusions of others while avoiding plagiarism and following a standard format for citation.

WHST.6-8.9

Draw evidence from informational texts to support analysis reflection, and research.

Range of Writing

WHST.6-8.10

Write routinely over extended time frames (time for reflection and revision) and shorter time frames (a single sitting or a day or two) for a range of discipline-specific tasks, purposes, and audiences.

Writing

http://www.corestandards.org/the-standards/english-language-arts-standards/writing-6-12/grade-8/

Text Types and Purposes

W.8.1

Write arguments to support claims with clear reasons and relevant evidence.

- Introduce claim(s), acknowledge and distinguish the claim(s) from alternate or opposing claims, and organize the reasons and evidence logically.
- Support claim(s) with logical reasoning and relevant evidence, using accurate, credible sources and demonstrating an understanding of the topic or text.
- Use words, phrases, and clauses to create cohesion and clarify the relationships among claim(s), counterclaims, reasons, and evidence.
- Establish and maintain a formal style.
- Provide a concluding statement or section that follows from and supports the argument presented.

W.8.2

Write informative/explanatory texts to examine a topic and convey ideas, concepts, and information through the selection, organization, and analysis of relevant content.

- Introduce a topic clearly, previewing what is to follow; organize ideas, concepts, and information into broader categories; include formatting (e.g., headings), graphics (e.g., charts, tables), and multimedia when useful to aiding comprehension.
- Develop the topic with relevant, well-chosen facts, definitions, concrete details, quotations, or other information and examples.
- Use appropriate and varied transitions to create cohesion and clarify the relationships among ideas and concepts.
- Use precise language and domain-specific vocabulary to inform about or explain the topic.
- Establish and maintain a formal style.
- Provide a concluding statement